# Vision at Patmos

A Study of the Book
of Revelation

# Vision at Patmos

## Catherine & Justo González

ABINGDON PRESS / NASHVILLE

VISION AT PATMOS:
A Study of the Book of Revelation

This book is printed on acid-free paper. 4/9 2

**Library of Congress Cataloging-in-Publication Data**

GONZÁLEZ, CATHERINE GUNSALUS.
  Vision at Patmos : study of the book of Revelation / by Catherine Gunsalus González and Justo Luis González.
    p.    cm. — (Abingdon lay Bible studies)
  Reprint. Originally published: United Methodist Church, 1977?
  **ISBN 0-687-43774-1** (pbk : alk. paper)
  1. Bible. N.T. Revelation—Criticism, interpretation, etc.
  I. González, Justo L. II. Title. III. Series.
BS2825.2.G65    1991
228'.06—dc20                                        90-37147
                                                        CIP

Originally published by the Women's Division of the Board of Global Ministries, The United Methodist Church.

# Preface

Bible study is one of the foundations of the Christian life. In the ancient church, however, very few Christians could study the Bible in private. There were two reasons for this. First, it is likely that not all Christians could read. Secondly, before the invention of the printing press, few people possessed entire manuscripts of the Bible. For these reasons, most Bible study took place in groups, generally as part of the worship service. The faithful gathered. Before communion, which was the center of the worship service, they heard a portion of the Bible read and explained.

Today we are in a different situation. Thanks to the invention of the printing press we can have our own copies of the Bible. We can study the Bible privately in our own homes. We can do this in the midst of our daily labors and therefore come to a deeper understanding of the word of God.

But this new situation also has its disadvantages. Most of the Bible was never intended to be studied privately. It was written to be read and studied in the midst of the congregation of God's people. For instance, if we read Paul's letters to the Corinthians, it is clear that he was writing these letters to be read to the congregation when they were gathered together. If we devote ourselves only to Bible study in private and never study God's word in a group, we will miss some of the message of the scriptures.

The same is true of the Book of Revelation. It was not written to be read in private but in the midst of the congregation. Therefore, the best means for studying it is in groups of Christians who gather in order to read and understand it together.

This book was originally written as a study resource for United Methodist Women. As such, part of the assignment was that our book should consist of six study sessions. It is possible, however, for a group to decide to spend more than one study session on any of the six chapters. In that case, the leader will need to make the necessary adjustments in the questions for discussion and the preparation for the next session.

The six studies are all written with the assumption that each member of the group would read the assigned portion of the Book of Revelation for each chapter. As you will see, the study does not follow the order of the Book of Revelation. However, if each of the assignments is read, the entire book will be studied. On page 6 there is a chart showing how the six chapters in this study book relate to the various sections in Revelation.

C.G.G. and J.L.G.
Decatur, Georgia
April, 1990

# The Structure of This Study Book

As you look at the Table of Contents, you will notice that this study book does not always follow the order in which various passages appear in the Book of Revelation. In order to organize this study book as six units, it was necessary to group various parts of Revelation under one heading. For instance, the first study deals with both the introduction and the conclusion of Revelation.

However, as you study the Table of Contents more carefully, you will also notice that, if for each study you read the biblical passages assigned, at the end of the six lessons you will have read the entire Book of Revelation.

The following outline will help you see how the six chapters of the study book relate to the Book of Revelation.

**Note:** Definitions of the words marked with an asterisk appear in the glossary.

| Chapters in Revelation | Themes | Chapters in Study Book |
|---|---|---|
| 1 | Introduction | I |
| 2<br>3 | Letters to the seven churches | II |
| 4<br>5<br>6 | The praise of God<br>The Lamb and the sealed scroll<br>The four horsemen and their woes | III |
| 7<br>8 }<br>9 }<br>10<br>11:1-14 | The glory of the martyrs<br>The trumpets of wrath<br>John eats the little scroll<br>The two witnesses | V |
| 11:15-19<br>12 | The last trumpet: God's triumph<br>The woman clothed with the sun | III |
| 13<br>14<br>15 }<br>16 }<br>17 }<br>18 } | The beasts from the sea and from the earth<br>The worshipers of the Lamb and of the Beast<br>The bowls of wrath<br>The fall of Babylon | IV |
| 19:1-10 | Hymns to God and the Lamb | V |
| 19:11-21 }<br>20 } | The victory of the Lamb | III |
| 21 }<br>22:1-5 } | The New Creation | VI |
| 22:6-21 | Conclusion | I |

8

# Contents

# 1
# An Open and Closed Letter

*Revelation 1:1-20; 22:6-21*

Few other books in the Bible have created as much controversy as the Revelation to John. Some people are attracted to it and find more meaning in it than in the gospels themselves. Others are repelled by it and avoid reading it. Some of the great scholars in the history of the church have written commentaries on all of the other books of the New Testament except Revelation. Others have created elaborate schemes for all of world history and the future on the basis of this one book, ignoring almost all the rest of the Bible. Neither extreme is very helpful. The Book of Revelation *is* a part of the Bible—even though in early times there was some opposition to its inclusion in the canon.

We must be familiar with Revelation, for it is God's word to us. At the same time, the book is a *part* of the Bible and must be seen and read within the context of the whole Bible. It ought not to be isolated and read by itself as the only scripture. We need to read and understand it in light of the rest of the Bible.

This chapter begins by suggesting that we read the opening and closing verses of the book. This is not to see how the story ends, but to see the unity, character and purpose of the book.

# The Author of Revelation

Revelation takes its name from the opening words: "The revelation of Jesus Christ ... to his servant John." It is a revelation *to* John, not a revelation *of* John. The Greek word for "revelation" is *apokalypsis,* so this book is often called The Apocalypse.*

Who was this John to whom this revelation was given? There has been a great deal of discussion and argument about this for at least the last eighteen hundred years! There are four other books in the New Testament which are said to be written by someone named John: The Gospel according to John and the First, Second, and Third Epistles of John. Were these all written by the same person? The Gospel includes words (John 21:20-25) in which the author said he was one of the original disciples of Jesus who was with him at the Last Supper. The First Epistle does not include any statement concerning its authorship. The Second and Third Epistles simply say that the author is "an elder," though no name is used. Yet many similarities in language and style and content make it reasonable to assume that one person might have written the gospel and the three epistles.

The same is not true of the Book of Revelation. Although the author said several times that his name was John, he never claimed to be an original disciple or an elder. The style of writing, the language used, cannot really be from the same pen that wrote the gospel and the epistles. We read all of the books in English; therefore we do not notice the differences in language that are obvious in the Greek. The author or authors of the Gospel and the Epistles of John wrote Greek in a good and standard fashion. The author of the Revelation was not natively Greek-speaking. His writing bears the marks of someone whose original language was Aramaic or Hebrew. He apparently made his own translations of various Old Testament passages from Hebrew into Greek.

Revelation tells us that John was in exile on the island of Patmos in the Aegean Sea, about sixty miles off the coast of Ephesus. According to the fourth century church historian Eusebius, John, the author of Revelation, was from the city of Ephesus and was sent into exile by order of the Emperor Domitian in A.D. 95. He was there for 18 months, until the next emperor, Nerva, ended his exile. The situation in which—and to which—the author of Revelation wrote is also a situation that is not apparent in the other Johannine writings. At the time Revelation was written, Rome was persecuting Christians.

## The Situation in which It Was Written

There have been various estimates throughout the centuries about when Revelation was written. The strongest arguments seem to point to the very end of the first century, about A.D. 95, which supports Eusebius' report. At that time (81-96), Domitian was the Roman Emperor. Toward the end of his reign there was a period of persecution of those who would not worship the Emperor as a god. We shall return to this theme later, when the political situation can be directly seen in particular passages in Revelation. In these opening verses, however, John identified himself as one who shared "with you in Jesus the tribulations." Indeed he was in exile because of his Christian witness (1:9).

# The Nature of Apocalyptic Literature

Even if we have never spent much time reading the Book of Revelation, we are probably aware that it is very different from other parts of scripture. It uses a great deal of symbolism.* It seems to say little about what was happening at the time and a great deal about what was going to happen in the future. And yet, it is not as easy to read as some of the Old Testament prophets who also talked about the future. Why is this book so different?

"The future" is a fairly indefinite term. It covers everything from the next moment to a million years from now. It covers everything in that time that can be· represented on a calendar. The term prophecy* generally refers to words that help interpret the present from God's point of view or that say something about a future time that is to come within our world and our history, a time that we can locate on our calendars. Many of the prophets in the Old Testament spoke about a future that was to be fairly soon, within the lifetime of the people who first heard the prophet (See, for example, Amos 2:4-16, Isaiah 43:1-7.). Some talked about a time in the more indefinite future.

Yet there is another kind of future to which the Bible also looks. It is a future which is at the end of our world and our history. It is the time of the Kingdom, the time when the rule of God will have no opposition and there will be no distance between God and creatures. It is the future that is at the end, when the goal of history and creation have been reached. This future is beyond all calendars. The general, technical term for this kind of future is *eschaton*, which is a Greek word meaning the end or goal. In English, when we talk about this absolute kind of future, we say we are talking about eschatology.*

Revelation is clearly eschatological literature.* It speaks about the ultimate and final future. But there is a further distinction that needs to be made. There is more than one type of eschatological literature. In reading Jeremiah 31:31-34 we can see a magnificient vision of this kind of future, yet the flavor of the passage is very different than what we find in most of the Book of Revelation. Both are eschatological, but Revelation is also apocalyptic literature.* This term comes from the same Greek word we mentioned earlier, *apokalypsis.* It means "revelation," and that is probably all that it meant at the time John wrote his book. Even then this word was becoming a technical term; it is that for us today. Apocalyptic literature contains revelations of the end time in the form of visions which the person who received them then puts into writing. The term apocalyptic is therefore used to describe certain parts of the Bible in which the term itself is not to be found. The most famous of these—and important for our study—is the Book of Daniel in the Old Testament.

The visions in apocalyptic literature have certain characteristics in common. Such writings arise in times of persecution; this helps to account for similarities. They are to be found in the Old and the New Testaments and also in both Jewish and Christian literature outside of the Bible. Because of the terrible reality of persecution, apocalyptic writers assume that the forces of evil are presently in charge of this world. In no way do they deny that God is good or that God is in control of everything and stronger than the forces of evil. Neither Judaism nor Christianity could agree to such denials. It asserts that the just and righteous— those who are truly God's people—must presently suffer. God allows this to happen because it is the final testing of the saints, the final unmasking of the evil forces. The end of the age is about to be ushered in. Apocalyptic literature explains why God allows the righteous and faithful ones to suffer. Such literature is always popular whenever people feel overwhelmed by evil forces and that they do not deserve such suffering. Apocalyptic writing answers the question: *Why does a good and powerful God allow such evil to go unchecked?* Apocalyptic literature replies to this question by saying that God has withdrawn from this world in order to test the faithful and give the unrighteous time to show their sinfulness. God intends to end this age very soon. Then judgment will come and the evil ones will be punished and the righteous ones will be rewarded. But the righteous must remain faithful even in the midst of the suffering and persecution which the unrighteous inflict on them now.

Other parts of the Bible also deal with suffering. They are not apocalyptic in that they do not conclude that God has given this world over to evil and is about to end the present age. The Book of Job is a classic example of wrestling with the same question of unjust suffering within the individual life; as is the brief Psalm 73. Psalm 44 suggests apocalypticism more because it deals with a situation of unjust persecution of the whole people of God and it appears to the psalmist that God is asleep, which is certainly a way of saying withdrawn from our world (Psalm 44:23). Yet the psalm is not apocalyptic, for it does not assert that the end of the age will be soon. The faith of the psalmist anticipated that the cries of God's people would indeed be answered within the present age.

Of course, the greatest point at which the question of the unjustified suffering of God's people is raised is at the cross itself. The first few verses of Revelation say about Jesus: "Behold, he is coming with the clouds, and every eye will see him, every one who pierced him" (1:7). Not only is the cross stressed but also the resurrection, for the One who was pierced is also "the firstborn of the dead" (1:5). Christ also was persecuted, and yet remained "the faithful witness" (1:5), even through suffering and death. John, in his visions, saw the task of Christians in his day to be "faithful witnesses" themselves, so that they also might share in the victory of Christ. The word "witness" which is used here is, in Greek, *martus*, from which our English word "martyr"* comes. At the time of the writing of Revelation, the word "martyr" was beginning to have a special meaning within the church. Because the faithful witnesses during persecutions in the early church were so often put to death, the word "witness" came to have the meaning of one who is put to death on account of the faith. In the centuries since then, "martyr" came to mean one who is put to death or persecuted because of what she or he believes.

## An Open Letter

John wrote to seven churches in "Asia." What he meant by Asia was Asia Minor, an area within the Roman Empire. Today all seven churches would fall within the country of Turkey. These seven churches were rather close together—less than 150 miles separated the farthest two. Ephesus is probably the city best known to us from this group since it figured so frequently in Paul's ministry. Christianity grew faster in Asia Minor than it did in any other area of the empire in those early days.

The persecutions under Domitian were especially severe in Asia Minor. Why was the empire attacking the Christians? The empire was not certain who the Christians were. Frequently the Christians were charged with "atheism" because they had no visible gods and also refused to worship the emperor. Obviously they were considered suspect by the state. The empire already knew of one group that refused to worship the emperor and had done so for generations—the Jews. An exception had been made grudgingly for them within the empire. Sometimes the Christians were all thought to be Jews. There was some basis for this, of course, since the earliest Christians were all Jews and the church had many ties, in scripture, theology, and practice with Judaism.

The empire had exempted Jews from the otherwise universal requirement of public worship of the emperor. This did not make them a favored people. Precisely their exemption caused them to be viewed with suspicion. There had been occasional insurrectionist activities within various Jewish communities, especially in Asia Minor, caused by a feeling that the time of the Messiah* was near. Many Jews had come to Asia Minor as refugees of the war that had taken place in Palestine between Jews and Romans in A.D. 66-70. Some Jews in Jerusalem had tried to free Israel from bondage to Rome. This attempt had failed utterly. The Roman legions finally entered Jerusalem and destroyed the city. Most particularly, they destroyed the Temple. Throughout this period and following the destruction of Jerusalem, the Jews in the Roman Empire felt keenly the power and oppression of Rome.

During this time, Jewish apocalyptic literature flourished. Many expected the end of Roman rule, complete with the promised Messiah. Rumors spread, excitement abounded, and Rome feared another Jewish uprising. Troops were sent in and many people were killed. By A.D. 95 there were such Jewish groups in Asia Minor. Furthermore, Christian groups there maintained many links with Judaism. There were also groups within the church that expected an imminent return of Jesus, the overthrow of Rome, and a new kingdom set up in Jerusalem. The Emperor Domitian was not sure of his power, so he increased demands that he be considered a god. He was a tyrant when there was any question of his authority. For this reason he began the persecution of Jews and Christians, particularly in Asia. He probably made little or no distinction between Jewish and Christian groups.

The parallel situation between Christians and Jews may be seen in the fact that, at about the same time as John was writing Revelation, a Jew was writing a similar book which is known as II Esdras.* This book reflects the same hostility to Rome which marks John's Revelation.

John's book was a letter to the churches of Asia, specifically the seven churches grouped in a circle near and including the city of Ephesus. The whole book was addressed to all of these churches and was expected to be read by all of them. This was definitely an "open letter." It was by no means a private communication!

John wrote: "Blessed is he who reads aloud the words of the prophecy" (1:3). He hardly meant that we would be blessed if we sat by ourselves in our homes and read the words of his book out loud! There is no particular virtue in that. To read aloud was to read in public. What John anticipated was that his book would be read out loud by the official reader when the church was gathered together. It was not possible for each Christian to have copies of various writings. So the church appointed readers. Frequently the reader would begin quite a while before the worship service in order that the people could gather to hear scripture read. At this time, scripture meant the Old Testament. But within the worship service the gospels were also being read—not all four in each church; but one or more in each. The letters of Paul had also been recently collected and were circulating in many churches. These writings were important in the worship and were read to the congregation. John may have visualized his letter to the churches having a similar role in his local area.

John may have had a specific understanding of the way his letter ought to be received and why it ought to be read out loud. At this time in the church's life there were those who were called "prophets." These people frequently spoke during the service and often interpreted current events in the light of God's promises.

Paul listed prophets just after apostles (I Cor. 12:28) when he spoke of the roles that are important in the church. Paul distinguished the prophet from one who spoke in tongues because the prophet instructed church members whereas the speaker in tongues had no message to give to others (I Cor. 14:1-5). Paul anticipated that the prophets would speak when the church gathered (I Cor. 14:26-33). It is not clear in Paul's writings how the function of prophesying in the church differed from today's preaching. Within apocalyptic circles, the prophesies may have taken on the character of visions. That is not a necessary part of Paul's definition of prophecy.

John may have been such a prophet from the church in Ephesus or from the general area. He seems to have had a sense of his own authority within those churches. John's visions occurred "on the Lord's day," when he normally would have been worshipping with the church. John said: "I was in the Spirit on the Lord's Day" (1:10). The work of the prophet was understood to be the result of the activity of the Spirit. All of this indicates that John's letter contained the words of prophecy he would have spoken to the churches had he been with them in person. Since he could not be there, the words were to be read by someone else in order that his presence as a prophet might be felt by the congregation.

Throughout the Book of Revelation, there is a setting of worship. Hymns abound in the visions. It is no accident that many of us are most familiar with various verses of Revelation from their musical settings, especially in Handel's *Messiah*. "The Hallelujah Chorus" and the anthem "Worthy is the Lamb that was Slain" both come from chapters in this book. The angels, the faithful, the elders, sing hymns to God and to Christ constantly in the book. There are also overtones of the baptismal service and of communion throughout.

We may find it strange that this vision is cast in such a liturgical or worship setting. In fact, we may be surprised that John's vision occurred when the congregation was gathered on Sunday. Were we to be in a similar situation—in exile, away from all the other church members we knew—we can imagine that we might indeed miss them and wish we were back with them.

But much more is involved here. First of all, John knew that life might not be any easier back in those churches since persecution was continuing. Any of those Christians could be in danger of death. He had no romantic desire to be back in a safe place. Secondly, for John and for his congregation, as was typical in the church at that time, worshipping together on Sunday was a necessary part of the Christian life. Even at the risk of persecution, they met each Sunday—the Lord's Day—in order to sing hymns, hear the readings and the messages, pray, and celebrate together the Lord's Supper, which was for them the sign that the Risen Lord was in their midst. This was the high point of the service every Sunday. Corporate worship was central to the Christian life in a way that we can scarcely imagine in our modern, individualistic way of thinking.

John knew he was still a part of that church. As they gathered for worship, he was with them. The vision he had was for them, not for himself. There is nothing in this letter that would support any idea that "I can be a Christian by myself."[1] Perhaps that is one reason why this book has not been particularly popular. We can take verses from the gospels or the letters of Paul and apply them to ourselves or model our lives on them without much of any sense that we *need* the community of the church. The early church would not have so understood these writings, but we are quite able to. Revelation is a different matter. The sense of Christian community, which is held together by baptism, communion and worship, runs throughout the book.

Not only did John address a community—all of the New Testament authors did that—he wrote as a part of the worship service. This setting pervades his whole message including the closing verses. In 22:20-21 are the words: "Come, Lord Jesus! The grace of the Lord

---

[1] This is the title of a hymn written by Richard Avery and Donald Marsh which includes this chorus:

*My heart's the church, my head's the steeple.*
*Shut the door and I'm the people.*
*I can be a Christian by myself.*

(Copyright 1972 by Richard K. Avery and Donald S. Marsh. From *The Avery and Marsh Songbook*. Used by permission of Proclamation Productions, Inc., Port Jervis, NY 12771.)

The words of the verses make it clear that such an attitude is not really possible for Christians.

Jesus be with all the saints. Amen." At first glance it may appear that these words refer to the hope of the second coming of Christ. Surely this is part of the meaning. But to any Christian reading or hearing these words in the late first or early second century, much more than this would have been involved. These are words that were used by the church at the communion meal. We find almost the same words at the close of Paul's First Letter to the Corinthians (I Cor. 16:22-23). In the early church writing called *The Didache** (10:6), these words also are given in the communion prayer. It is also interesting to note that in all three cases—Revelation, I Corinthians, *The Didache*—this brief prayer and benediction occurs with a statement about those who are to be cursed. Some such words evidently were also part of the communion service. In the case of Revelation, the curses are to fall on any who tamper with John's words of prophecy.

The words translated "Come, Lord Jesus!" are Aramaic, one of the languages of Palestine, rather than Greek. This expression, *Maranatha,** is ancient in the life of the church. It means "Our Lord, Come!" or "Our Lord comes!" or "Our Lord has come!" Its use in the communion service would refer both to the real but veiled presence of the Lord known to us in the breaking of bread and to the future coming of the Lord at the end of the present age. These two events were inseparable for the early church. Today we tend to read these closing verses differently from the way the author or the original readers would have understood them. Because most of us do not use the phrase, "Come, Lord Jesus," in our present-day celebrations of the Lord's Supper, we have lost much of the sense of the unique presence of Christ with the church in the sacrament.

John wrote an "open letter" to the seven churches in Asia. It was open because it was to be read in public worship. It was a general letter to the Christians who were suffering under the persecution of the Roman Empire. It was not a private communication to one person or something to be heard by a select few.

## A Closed Book

Revelation is also a "closed book" to modern readers. It is, for the most part, cryptic. It uses a kind of code language, so we cannot be sure what is meant at every point. This is also typical of apocalyptic writing.

There are basically two reasons why apocalyptic literature is cryptic. The first is that most apocalyptic literature is in the form of visions. We may not be sure what a vision really is, for most of us do not have visions of any sort. Yet we know that in every generation there are people who do—people who are in touch with the world and are mentally healthy. Many of the great mystics in the history of the church have had such experiences. Of course there are other people who have less contact with reality and who are not so healthy who also have visions. The church always has the task of distinguishing visions with a true message from visions that corrupt and falsify the Gospel. Not all visions are from God. Just as there can be false prophets, there can be false visionaries.

Visions are a sort of "waking dream." Visions have many of the characteristics of dreams that we all have when we are asleep. Dreams are, in themselves, a cryptic form of communication we carry on with ourselves. Throughout history there have been attempts to interpret dreams, because their meanings are not obvious, even to the dreamer. Scenes suddenly shift; one thing is transformed into another; a person becomes someone else; animals enter and leave and change their shapes and sizes. We are used to this in dreams, so it ought not to surprise us that visions often show the same tendency.

The second reason Revelation is cryptic is that the author, quite consciously, wanted to write his message in a hidden fashion. The church was being persecuted by the empire. Part of the reason for persecution was the belief that people who refused to worship the emperor were traitors to the state and might even be part of a subversive group. Had the ideas of this book circulated openly—ideas that included seeing the emperor as a demonic force, the personification of evil—surely the Christians would have been considered even more to be traitors. So these thoughts were written in such a way as to hide, partly, the meaning from those outside the church. No names of emperors were used, yet an emperor was obviously intended. Rome was called "Babylon," so that no offense could be taken by a Roman official. The situation of persecution dictated that the political character of this book could not be spelled out clearly. Only readers familiar with the Old Testament could have understood the political sentiments of the book.

Our task in these next few studies will be to thread our way through some of the strange and dreamlike material of Revelation and see what John had to reveal to the churches of Asia. Beyond this, we need to see what this portion of God's word has to say to us today. We are in a radically different situation. Our churches are not under persecution. Yet, as the body of Christ, we ought to suffer along with those members of the body where there is persecution of the church. Even without persecution, there is in this book a call to faithfulness that is valid in all times and places.

This is, indeed, very strange material, but we should not avoid it for that reason. Above all, we need to study this book, peculiar as it is, within the wider context of the whole biblical message. This apocalypse was included within the New Testament, not because it contained material that was absolutely foreign and different from everything else. It was included because, even with its strangeness, the church recognized the familiar voice of its Lord and the Gospel.

# Studying This Chapter

## Purpose of the Chapter

Our purpose in this opening chapter is to give some basic information about the Book of Revelation, such as authorship, date, the situation in which it was written and the nature of apocalyptic writing.

## Questions and Suggested Methods

1) Because of the radically different attitudes that Christians have toward the Book of Revelation, begin by asking what each member of the group knows about the book or what each one feels about the book. Where has (s)he learned about it? Is each one looking forward to studying it, or does (s)he dread getting into such peculiar material? If the group is too large for this exercise, ask a representative panel from the group to give its views.

2) Imagine that you are part of a church during a time of persecution. You are subject to arrest and even death if known by the government to be part of such a congregation. Write a message to another such congregation that tells them to have courage and maintain their faithfulness, that the government will not last forever and God will vindicate those who are now suffering. Do this in such a manner that the other congregation will understand, and yet the government will not, should the message be intercepted. You may take for granted that the government does not know the Bible. If the group is large enough, divide, and have them send messages to each other.

3) There are other portions of the Bible that are apocalyptic. Ask some members of the group, in advance, to read the following passages and bring to the group a brief summary of their contents: Daniel ch. 7—8; Daniel ch. 10—12; Matthew 24; Mark 13; Luke 21:5-36. Help the group, after the reports, to make a list of the common features of all of these passages.

4) In Chapter One there have been comments about the general character of dreams which may help us understand the symbolism of visions a little better from our own experience. You may wish to have some discussion of this, based on the group's own knowledge of dreaming.

There is another analogy that can be made with visions and the poetic imagination. Great poetry often conveys truth to us, and yet the poem cannot be easily analyzed and dissected. An absolutely agreed upon meaning cannot be determined. The imagery* and construction of the poem make the words say more than those same words say in another context. For example, here is a famous poem by Emily Dickinson (1830-1886):

> After great pain, a formal feeling comes—
> The Nerves sit ceremonious, like Tombs—
> The stiff Heart questions was it He, that bore,
> And Yesterday, or Centuries before?
>
> The Feet, mechanical, go round—
> Of Ground, or Air, or Ought—
> A Wooden way
> Regardless grown,
> A Quartz contentment, like a stone—
>
> This is the Hour of Lead—
> Remembered, if outlived,
> As Freezing persons, recollect the Snow—
> First—Chill—then Stupor—then the letting go—

This is the entire poem. Ask the group to read it and see if it can feel the poem's meaning. Then try to analyze the meaning of the words. Write the same message in regular sentences without using imagery. If the group is large, divide and compare results.

## Preparing for the Next Study

The first lesson has been an introduction to the strange literature that is to be studied, complete with visions and words that are mystifying. However, the lesson for next time—the second and third chapters of Revelation—deals with some of the most familiar material of this unfamiliar book. These chapters contain the "letters to the seven churches." Some of the verses will be ones we can all quote though we may not have known they came from Revelation.

Ask group members to note the verses that are very familiar to them as they read the two chapters of Revelation assigned for the next study. These can then be shared at the beginning of the next meeting. Ask them to state where or when this verse came to their attention, such as in a musical setting or on a stained-glass window. In addition, to prepare for one of the suggested methods for study in the next lesson, ask several members of the group to collect four or five stories in newspapers or church periodicals that tell about problems faced by churches in several different parts of the world.

Emily Dickinson's poem, "After great pain," is from *The Complete Poems of Emily Dickinson*, edited by Thomas H. Johnson. By permission of Little, Brown, and Co.

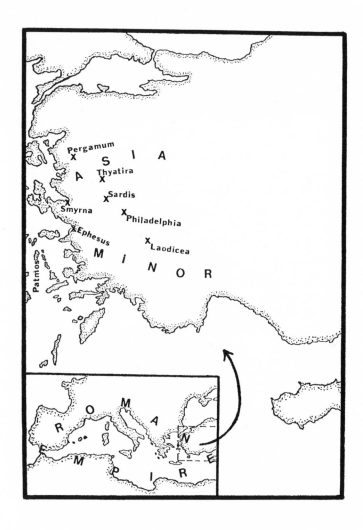

# 2
# Seven Shared Messages

*Revelation 2:1-3:22*

As we saw in the previous study, the book of Revelation is like an open letter to the churches in Asia Minor. And yet, the second and third chapters contain what appears to be a collection of seven letters to just as many churches in that region. Our inclination would be to think of these letters as private communications from the seer of Patmos to each of these churches. But that would be wrong. There is nothing to indicate that these letters were written as separate units or that they circulated as such until they were compiled. The epistles of Paul circulated separately, but the seven "letters" which appear in Revelation 2 and 3 always circulated together.

This means that these "letters" were not private messages sent to each of the churches. They were a means to focus the book on the situations and the needs of each of these Christian communities. The book was intended to be read in public in all the churches in the region. Thus, the Christians in Ephesus would hear not only the message addressed directly to them but also the ones sent to Smyrna, Sardis, and the rest. The result would be twofold: *first,* it would be clear that there was a common bond uniting all these communities into one. *Secondly,* the message of the whole book would come to sharper focus on the specific needs of each local church, for each had heard itself addressed in concrete terms.

John's use of the number "seven" was a way of addressing *all* the churches. The seven churches—or seven stars, or seven lampstands—were a way of referring at once to those specific seven churches, and to the entire church. In biblical usage, the number* seven means that something is complete, perfect, fulfilled. This is the significance of creation in seven days. There are literally hundreds of other instances in which the number seven is used in that sense. Therefore, the fact that letters were addressed to seven churches does not mean that the book was addressed only to them, nor that they were the only Christian communities in Asia Minor. As a matter of fact, there were probably many other churches which must have existed in that general area at the same time. It would be odd for the Spirit to address only these seven churches, as if no others existed.

The unity of all these churches is symbolized in several common features which appear in all the letters:

1. The first of these features is that each letter is addressed to "the angel of the church in . . ."

There have been several different interpretations of what is meant here by "angel." Some have thought that what we have here is the influence of Persian religion, where each person had a guardian angel. This is highly unlikely for the "angel" addressed here shared in both the praise and the blame for behavior in its church. In any case, it is difficult to see what could be the point of addressing such an angel when, in fact, the message was clearly directed to the church. Probably the meaning is much simpler than that. The word "angel" in Greek means "messenger."

It is therefore quite likely that the letters were sent to the churches, in form at least, through their leaders. These leaders, as shepherds of the flock, were, in a sense, responsible for all that happened in the congregation. For this reason, the letters in some cases chastized them for things which clearly were not their own individual faults. The leaders were not really being blamed for the shortcomings of their flocks; their tasks and responsibilities were being pointed out to them.

2. The second feature is that all these letters begin with a statement about the One whose message is being communicated.

● The letter to the Ephesians comes from *him who holds the seven stars in his right hand, who walks among the seven golden lampstands* (2:1).

Similar statements open the other letters:

● *The words of the first and the last, who died and came to life* (2:8).

● *The words of him who has the sharp two-edged sword* (2:12).

● *The words of the Son of God, who has eyes like a flame of fire, and whose feet are like burnished bronze* (2:18).

● *The words of him who has the seven spirits of God and the seven stars* (3:1).

● *The words of the holy one, the true one, who has the key of David, who opens and no one shall shut, who shuts and no one opens* (3:7).

● *The words of the Amen, the faithful and true witness, the beginning of God's creation* (3:14).

All of this is more than mere formula. It is typical of the entire book of Revelation. The messages which John sent to the churches were to be accepted, not because they stood on their own merits nor even on John's authority, but because they came from the Lord of the church. They were intimately connected with the power, character, and deeds of that Lord. In some cases, it is clear that these opening words center on an aspect of the work of Christ which is of particular significance for the situation of the church in question. In other cases that connection—if there is any—is not all that clear. But we shall deal with that question as we discuss each of the letters separately.

3. Finally, all seven letters, after delivering their message, end with the same exhortation: "Those who have ears, let them hear what the Spirit says to the churches" (Rev. 2:7, 11, 17, 29; 3:6, 13, 22).

Again, this was not just an empty formula. It placed the responsibility on the shoulders of the recipients of the message. The only excuse anyone could adduce for not responding to what the Spirit had to say was that (s)he had no ears. Obviously, any who had ears and did not listen had no excuse.

This formula was used to link together the messages to all the churches. We might expect the letters to call for each church to hear the message. But the term used was churches. Each was to hear and heed the word that was spoken to all the other churches as well as to itself. Again, these seven letters were not intended as separate, private communications, but rather as one shared message under seven concrete headings.

# The Letter to Ephesus

Ephesus was one of the richest cities of the ancient world. Located on a harbor at the tip of Asia Minor, it was a center of trade and travel. Within the structure of the Roman Empire, it was granted the status and limited autonomy of a free city.* Its markets and warehouses were filled with goods from various parts of the empire. Its people were proud of their city.

Nothing, however, was as much a source of pride for the Ephesians as was the temple of Diana, one of the seven wonders of the world. Its base was almost 100,000 square feet, and the entire structure was 60 feet high. In its midst stood the ancient statue of Diana (Artemis in Greek), which was said to have fallen from heaven. The statue, a representation of Diana as the source of fertility and abundance, was covered with many breasts. From all parts of the Mediterranean world, tourists and devotees came to view and to worship in this great temple.

The commercial interests in Ephesus were closely connected with worship. The temple of Diana, being a most sacred place, was used for the safekeeping of money and other assets, much as our modern-day banks. And in Acts 19:23-29 is a fascinating account of that connection between religion and financial interests. When the silversmiths see their industry threatened, they rally under the cry of "Great is Artemis of the Ephesians!"

The early life of the church in Ephesus is described in the book of Acts. Actually, in no other city did Paul work as long as he did in Ephesus. It is also there that we first hear of the famous preacher Apollos and of how Priscilla and her husband Aquila corrected his view of the Gospel (Acts 18:24-28). It seems that the church in Ephesus was a sizeable and lively community.

To this church there was a message of both praise and warning. It was praised because, in the midst of persecution, it was "enduring patiently and bearing up for my name's sake," and had "not grown weary" (Rev. 2:3). It was also praised because it had rejected some who had falsely claimed to be apostles (Rev. 2:2), and because it hated "the works of the Nicolaitans" (Rev. 2:6).[1]

On the other hand, however, this church was accused of having abandoned the love that it originally had, and warned that if it did not repent the Lord would take its lampstand from its place (Rev. 2:4-5). It would no longer be counted among the churches of Christ. Unfortunately, it is impossible to know what was meant by having abandoned the first love. It may have meant that the church had lost its original fervor in its love for Christ. It may also have meant that, in its efforts to stamp out the false apostles and the Nicolaitans, the church had lost its original spirit of love for other Christians. It may even have been that the church had begun to hate those who persecuted it and had lost the love it was to have for its enemies. Whatever may have been meant, it is clear that the message was the same as that of the opening verses of I Corinthians 13: without love, nothing else is of great value.

In any case, the church at Ephesus was to find both strength and warning in the fact that the One who sent this message held "the seven stars [that is, the entire church] in his right hand" and also walked "among

---

[1] See the section on the letter to Pergamum for more information on the Nicolaitans.

the seven golden lampstands" (Rev. 2:1)—that is, was present in the life of the church.

## The Letter to Smyrna

Smyrna too was a center of commerce and a free city. As a matter of fact, it often was a rival of Ephesus for the commerce of the area, as well as for honors and prestige.

Like Ephesus, Smyrna was noted for its pagan worship. In Smyrna, worship took forms which were potentially more dangerous for the church. These forms were the cults of Rome and the emperor. Most subjects of the Roman Empire were relatively happy with their condition. Rome had brought a measure of peace, a welcome relief after years of constant instability and war. The roads had been cleared of brigands and the sea of pirates. Commerce flourished. Famine could be averted in one place by shipping grain from other parts of the empire. Furthermore, since Rome was tolerant of local custom and freedom, its yoke was not often resented. As a result of these good conditions, many of Rome's subjects soon began worshipping the goddess Roma and the emperor. In both of these cults, Smyrna led the way. Almost three hundred years before the time of Revelation, it built the first temple in the world dedicated to Roma. Seventy years before John's exile, the city built a magnificent temple to the emperor. Ever since, it had been a center of the worship of both Rome and Caesar.

Precisely the issue of the cult of the emperor had precipitated the persecution. Domitian was unsure of the loyalty of his subjects—probably with good cause—therefore emperor worship became an important political issue. We can imagine the violence of persecution in a city as devoted to that cult as Smyrna was.

To the church in Smyrna, John wrote only words of comfort. This was not an easy comfort. For "ten days"—that is, a relatively short period—there would be tribulation. This may also be a reference to the time of testing in Daniel 1:12-15. But the one "who died and came to life" (Rev. 2:8) knew of their tribulation and poverty and of the slander against them. By being faithful unto death, the church would receive its crown and would not be "hurt by the second death" (Rev. 2:11). The image here is of the athlete who wins a race and receives a laurel wreath.

A phrase which is difficult to interpret is the reference to "the slander of those who say they are Jews and are not, but are a synagogue of Satan" (Rev. 2:9). On one hand, this may indicate early hostility between the Christians and the Jews. The Christians may have considered the Jews to be the cause of their persecution. There is evidence that both Jews and Christians were persecuted at that time. Many Christians saw themselves as the true Jews and therefore saw the others as false ones. On the other hand, the words may refer to false teachers, false apostles, Nicolaitans and followers of Balaam, who are repeatedly attacked in the other letters and may have been part of the internal problem of the church in Smyrna as well.

## The Letter to Pergamum

Pergamum was the provincial capital. Before that, it had been the capital of a vast kingdom whose last king had bequeathed it to Rome. This city was the center both of imperial power and cult. That is why it was called the place "where Satan's throne is" (Rev. 2:13). Some have seen in this phrase an allusion to the temple of Zeus, which was situated on a hill and might be compared to a throne. But John was probably referring to the fact that this city was the seat of Roman power in the area and therefore the symbol of the satanic powers which were loose upon the earth.

Apart from its political importance, Pergamum was also famous for its magnificent library. As a matter of fact, when its rivalry with Alexandria for the possession of the best library in the world broke into open hostility, Egypt stopped all shipments of papyrus to its rival. Pergamum then began using animal skins for copying its books. This material from Pergamum was given the name of "parchment"—that is, writing material from Pergamum. Most of the ancient manuscripts of the New Testament are written on parchment.

To the church set in that city, a message was sent from the One "who has the sharp two-edged sword" (Rev. 2:12). This is a reference to the coming victory and judgment of Christ. On the positive side of this message, there was the steadfastness of this church, as exemplified by Antipas, who was killed for the faith. He was a martyr, which at that time meant "witness" but was beginning to mean "one who suffered for the faith."

On the negative side, however, there were false doctrines which had spread among the faithful. "The teaching of Balaam" is a reference to the Old Testament figure who is the prototype of all the false teachers who have led Israel astray (Num. 31:16). The Christians at Pergamum were told that they, like the Ephesians, had "some who hold the teachings of the

Nicolaitans" (Rev. 2:15). According to certain Jewish writers of the time, "Balaam" and "Nicolaus" both meant "destroyer of the people." Therefore, John was saying that, as in times of old, there was a teaching which was destroying the people by inciting them to compromise with idolatry. In this context, the word "fornication" (KJV) or "immorality" (RSV) probably has the symbolic meaning, common in the Old Testament, of leaving the true God and committing adultery by following idols.

Here again, there is a promise for those who stand firm against both persecution and false teachings: "hidden manna," probably a reference to communion and to the heavenly banquet to which communion points, and "a white stone, with a new name written," probably a reference to a much more powerful protection than those amulets or charms that many pagans wore around their necks. There was also a Jewish tradition that manna had been stored in the Temple before its destruction and that it would remain hidden until the Temple could be rebuilt. Within this context, the "hidden manna" may be another reference to the coming kingdom, when the citizens would eat manna at the heavenly banquet.

## The Letter to Thyatira

Unlike the previous three cities, Thyatira was not an impressive town. It had no political significance and very little of which to be proud. Since it stood at an important crossroad and in a place not well-suited for defense, it had been captured and destroyed several times.

Thyatira's importance was due precisely to its location at the crossroad. It was a commercial town, where there were many traders and artisans. Ancient records indicate that, due to the nature of its livelihood, Thyatira had more craftsmen's guilds than many larger cities and that these guilds wielded significant power. As was true throughout the ancient world, these guilds combined some of the features of our modern trade unions with other religious features. Individuals had to belong to one of them in order to practice a certain trade. In order to belong to them, laborers had to participate in their meetings and ceremonies. These meetings often took place in pagan temples, where an animal was offered to the gods and then eaten by the members of the guild.

This obviously put Christians in a difficult dilemma. If they did not participate in such feasts and ceremonies, they would be unable to make a living. If they did participate, they were being unfaithful to the Lord.

In this situation, teachings such as those in Pergamum must have seemed very attractive. Perhaps it would be acceptable for Christians to participate in the pagan ceremonies as long as they remained a Christian inside. The leader of those who proposed this easy way out was a woman called "Jezebel." It is highly unlikely that this was her real name, for no Christian or Jew would name a daughter that after the events told in I Kings. Just as in the previous letter the people with similar views were likened to Balaam, here this woman was described as a new Jezebel.

Jezebel called herself a prophetess. There were women prophetesses—women who preached— within the early church (see Acts 21:8-9). The prophetess of Thyatira was not condemned because she was a woman but because her teachings and her claim to being a prophetess were false. In this letter also, the terms "immorality" and committing adultery "with her" probably do not mean that this woman and her followers were immoral but rather that they were committing adultery against God.

In contrast to the adulterers, those who hear and obey the words of the One "who has eyes like a flame of fire" (Rev. 2:18) will receive "power over the nations" (Rev. 2:26).

## The Letter to Sardis

Sardis was a rich city. In ancient times, almost seven centuries before John's exile, it had been the capital of the famous Croesus. Although it was no longer a dazzlingly rich and powerful city, it still retained some of its old glory. Since five important roads met in Sardis, its trade was as active as that of Thyatira. Besides, its seemingly impregnable position atop a cliff made it an important military outpost. Finally, since the surrounding area was particularly well-suited for raising sheep, Sardis was a center for the wool trade, as well as for making cloth.

Very little that is positive is said to Sardis. In fact, the message of the letter can be summarized in its opening statement: "You have the name of being alive, and you are dead" (Rev. 3:1). This is striking since there is no mention of any of the difficulties mentioned in the other letters. There is no reference to persecutions, nor to pressure from the community, nor even to false doctrines within the church. On the contrary, everything seems to be running smoothly. Precisely that smoothness seems to have been the great tragedy of the church in Sardis. Its easy life was its greatest difficulty.

Yet even in the midst of that church there were still a few who had not "soiled their garments" (3:4). This image is probably a triple reference, having to do with the cloth trade for which Sardis was famous, with the theme of ritual uncleanness which appears throughout the Old Testament, and with the white garments in which Christians were robed as they emerged from baptism. These "shall walk with me in white" is another reference to the baptismal robe. Although the lot of the others is not spelled out, one may surmise that it is not a happy one.

## The Letter to Philadelphia

Philadelphia was less important than most of the other six cities. Its main source of wealth was the volcanic plains near it, where excellent vineyards flourished. For that reason, its main religious allegiance was to Dionysius, god of wine. But Philadelphia was also famous for its many other shrines. Though none were as great or as beautiful as the temple of Artemis in Ephesus, they nevertheless made an impressive collection. According to some authors, there was a custom of inscribing the name of great citizens on the pillars of these temples. This custom may be the background for the promise in 3:12: "He who conquers, I will make him a pillar in the temple of my God."

The letter to the Philadelphians is similar to the letter to Smyrna, for in both there are only positive words about the life and faith of the church in question. Also, in both we find the cryptic reference to "the synagogue of Satan." Unlike the letter to Smyrna, however, there is little or no mention of persecution. The phrase, "the hour of trial which is coming on the whole world" (3:10), seems to refer to the final calamities which the whole world shall suffer and not to persecution against Christians.

Finally, an interesting detail must be mentioned for it illustrates the nature of visions—that they cannot be taken as literal descriptions. The Christians of Philadelphia were told that they would be pillars in the temple of the heavenly city (3:12). Later, John said that there would be no temple in that city (21:22). This illustrates the figurative and poetic nature of visions and shows that any attempt to apply closely knit logical schemes to this book necessarily misinterprets the book itself.

## The Letter to Laodicea

Like so many of the cities mentioned in these two chapters of Revelation, Laodicea was a rich city. It was proud of its power and prosperity. When the city was destroyed by an earthquake in A.D. 60, the Roman authorities offered financial assistance. The Laodiceans refused all aid and insisted on rebuilding their city with their own resources. They did so. By the end of the century, when John wrote Revelation, Laodicea was again a prosperous city.

The sources of that prosperity were several, but two among them seem to be significant for understanding the letter addressed to the Christians in Laodicea. One of these was wool. A beautiful bluish black, it was coveted for its lustrous sheen. This was such an important factor in the life of Laodicea that the city itself was sometimes named after some of its dark woolen products. With this as background, it appears that in Revelation 3:18 the "white garments" of baptism contrast with dark woolen garments, one of the sources of the Laodiceans' pride.

The other significant product of Laodicea was a world-famous eye salve. This was shipped in tablets which the user would then break up, dissolve and put in his or her eyes. Again referring to that which was well-known to Laodiceans, John counseled Christians there to buy from Christ "salve to anoint your eyes, that you may see" (3:18).

Laodicea had very few problems with anything or anyone besides itself. The case of Laodicea was even worse than that of Sardis. In the letter to Sardis, some were excepted from the harsh words, whereas in Laodicea all were given the same sharp rebuke.

There was still hope for Laodicea, for Christ was standing at the door and knocking; some could still be conquerors with him (3:20-21).[2] But that hope was an offer more than an indication that some in Laodicea were on the right track.

What was the great sin of the Laodiceans which caused Christ, "the faithful and true witness," to say that he would spew them out of his mouth? Literally, nothing. Their sin was not something that they did or thought. It was not even something they decided not to do. It was rather a comfortable, middle-of-the-road lukewarmness. At a time when God was doing great things, at a time when the church was pitched in mortal combat against the powers of evil, they were lukewarm. They were contented and smug. Thus the Lord said to them: "You say, I am rich, I have prospered, and I need nothing; not knowing that you are wretched, pitiable, poor, blind and naked" (3:17).

## A Letter to Us

All of the foregoing may be very interesting information about the churches in Asia Minor at the

---

[2] Note that in the reference to Christ's presence at the door, the imagery of the communion service is clear, for Christ will come in and eat with them.

end of the first century. But, if we believe we are studying God's word to us, we are studying it not simply because it conveys interesting information but rather because it speaks to us today and calls us to obedience.

What do these letters say to us today? To answer that question, we must note that the conditions of the seven churches were not all alike. Although most of them were struggling against persecution, some were tempted to compromise with the powers of evil. Others were seated smugly on the sidelines, watching the action and being happy that they were not touched by it. But the unity of the book and the seven shared messages to the churches show that, as the body of Christ, the various communities were facing a common struggle. None could claim to be apart from it.

This is significant for us because, once again, the churches throughout the world are facing different situations. Some are persecuted; their members are being added to the long list of Christian martyrs. Others are living in conditions of social injustice and are involved in a difficult struggle to change those conditions. Others, like the church in Laodicea, are rich, respected and safe. To all of these the Book of Revelation speaks, and its first word is that we are still one body. We must use our ears to "hear what the Spirit says to the churches"—to all of them, rich and poor, weak and powerful, secure and persecuted.

Of all the situations described in the seven letters, that of Laodicea probably fits most of us in the United States best. We live in a country which controls a large share of the wealth of the world. In this country, being a Christian seems to create no great conflicts with society. The threat of persecution seems quite distant. While there are still grave issues of social justice to be corrected, we have courts of law and other government agencies through which we can work. Therefore, when it comes to the struggle of good and evil throughout the world, our greatest temptation is to sit comfortably in our homes and pews and try to convince ourselves that we are not involved in that struggle. That was precisely the temptation of the church in Laodicea, and the words to them could be addressed to us: "You say, I am rich, I have prospered, and I need nothing; not knowing that you are wretched, pitiable, poor, blind and naked."

We must remember that we are all one body. In order to hear what the Spirit says to us, we must listen to what the Spirit says to the churches in Uganda, in Korea, in Bolivia, in Namibia and in our own ghettoes.

## Studying This Chapter

### Purpose of the Chapter

The purpose of the second chapter is to broaden our perspective of Revelation. When interpreting the Book of Revelation, there is a tendency to over-simplify its context and, therefore, its meaning. It is true that the book deals mainly with a situation of persecution but we must not allow the dramatic nature of that situation to overshadow everything else. John himself did not allow this to happen to his own perspective. In these letters there are several references to persecutions, but the letters are concerned also with less dramatic evils such as lukewarmness, false teachings and lack of love. This broader perspective allows us to see the relevance of the entire book to situations such as ours, where the evil at hand is not as obvious as persecution.

Another purpose of this chapter is to call us to "hear what the Spirit says to the churches." The letters to the seven churches, taken as a whole, constitute a unique reminder of the unity of the church, despite the different situations with which it must deal in various places.

## Questions and Suggested Methods

1) Persecution was one of the forms of evil threatening the churches to which the seven letters were written. What are some other forms of evil mentioned in the letters? As a group, make a list. The purpose of this list is not necessarily to pinpoint these various problems, but rather to broaden the group's perspective of the context of the Book of Revelation. There are some cases, such as Jezebel's "immorality" in Thyatira or the loss of love in Ephesus, in which there can be different conjectures concerning the exact nature of the problems in a given church. But it is still possible to make a generally accurate list of the evils confronting the seven churches.

2) As you read the letters to the seven churches and the commentary on them, keep in mind what you have read recently in newspapers and church publications about the situation of churches in different parts of the world. Distribute among the group the clippings that have been collected. Then try to relate them to the letters to the seven churches. Are there some elements in the seven letters that seem to apply to those

settings better than to us? Discuss this in a group. Avoid being judgmental about churches in situations different from ours. Rather, ask the question: What is the Spirit saying to the churches and, therefore, to us in these situations? Is there something we can learn from those churches?

3) Is it true that the letter to Laodicea applies best to us? To what degree is this true of North American Christianity as a whole? To what degree is it true of our local church? If any of this is true, what is the concrete meaning, in this situation, of the oft quoted verse (Rev. 3:20): "Behold, I stand at the door and knock; if any one hears my voice and opens the door, I will come in to him and eat with him, and he with me"? What would it mean, in the church of Laodicea, to "open the door"? What would it mean in our church?

## Preparing for the Next Study

Because the next study includes several symbolic elements about which there has been much discussion, ask three members of the class each to use a different commentary and make notes of the comments on the following passages:

1) 6:1-8 (the Four Horsemen)
2) 12:1-2 (the Woman in Childbirth)
3) 20:1-10 (the Millenium)*

Suggested commentaries for this purpose would be: The Interpreter's Bible, volume XII; G. B. Caird's The Revelation of St. John the Divine; and Minear's I Saw a New Earth (pp. 74-83; 122; 160-63). Further information on these books is to be found in the "For Further Study" section at the end of this study book.

These three "reporters" should then be prepared to give a brief summary of what each commentary said when the passages are discussed in the following meeting.

# 3

# The Victory
# of the Lamb

*Revelation 4:1-6:17; 11:15-12:17; 19:11-20:15*

With this chapter of our study we begin the visionary, classically apocalyptic portion of the Book of Revelation. In this and the next two studies we will be dealing with the material in Revelation 4:1—20:15. Because of the complex character and the length of this biblical material, we shall study it in terms of themes, rather than chapter by chapter. Three of the major themes that run through Revelation 4—20 are:

1. the victory gained by Jesus Christ,
2. the powers of evil now active in the world,
3. the struggle of the faithful in the face of evil.

These will be our themes in the third, fourth and fifth of our studies.

It probably seems strange that we should begin this series of three studies with the one of the victory of Christ. Surely it would make more sense to talk about evil first, then the struggle against evil, and finally, the victory of Christ over evil. What sense does it make to speak of the victory first and then of the struggle after that?

This question puts us into the heart of both the

beauty and the difficulty of the Book of Revelation. The sequence of events is not like that of the typical novel or drama. In fact, it is frequently difficult to discover the exact order of events even within the book itself. For this reason, there have been so many different theories about what Revelation says concerning the end of the age.

Imagine a two-level stage in a theatre. Some things are happening upstairs that clarify events downstairs, even though the people downstairs cannot see it. Sometimes the action upstairs shows what is soon to happen downstairs. Sometimes it is a reaction to and interpretation of what has already happened below. Therefore, the sequence of events is not clear. In the Book of Revelation John was giving the Christians of his time glimpses of what he thought was going on upstairs—in heaven—to help interpret and make sense of what was happening downstairs—on the earth. Because of the book's split-level characteristic, we can expect some difficulty in arranging the whole book into a neat, chronological order.

Probably the central picture in Revelation of the action in heaven is that God is, at last, going to destroy all the enemies of the faithful that have thwarted the fulfillment of the purposes God has for creation. For some time—in fact, ever since sin and disobedience entered into human history—these forces of evil have appeared to be victorious over God's plans. But, at long last, God is going to put an end to these alien powers. And Christ, the Lamb, is central in this victory of God.

## The Temporary Reign of Evil

The visionary scenes begin in chapter four with an incomparable picture of God's throne in heaven

(4:2-8). We are probably more familiar with these words in the hymn setting, "Holy, Holy, Holy! Lord God Almighty" *(The United Methodist Hymnal, #64).* God has always been powerful, totally ruling the world. God created the world. Whatever has come into existence remains under the control of God. Evil has been allowed, not because God was powerless against it, but because God wished that it be given room and time to operate within the world.

Why did God allow that which is contrary to the divine purpose to have apparently free rein within the world? The Book of Revelation does not give a direct answer to this question. There are, however, two considerations from the point of view of the whole biblical message. The first is that God's refusal to eliminate evil at once is often referred to as the divine patience or forbearance and is considered to be one of God's greatest characteristics:

> *The Lord is merciful and gracious,*
> *   slow to anger and abounding in steadfast love.*
> *He will not always chide,*
> *   nor will he keep his anger for ever.*
> *He does not deal with us according to our sins,*
> *   nor requite us according to our iniquities.*
> *For as the heavens are high above the earth,*
> *   so great is his steadfast love toward those who fear*
> *      him;*
> *as far as the east is from the west,*
> *   so far does he remove our transgressions from us.*
>                           (Psalm 103:8-12)

In his letter to the Romans, Paul said: "Do you presume upon the riches of [God's] kindness and forbearance and patience? Do you not know that God's kindness is meant to lead you to repentance?" (Romans 2:4).

When we recognize ourselves to be sinful, then God's patience is a characteristic we celebrate—and rightly so. However, in a time of great tribulation and persecution, when Christians can with justification see themselves on God's side over against the powers of evil, God's forbearance of evil is not seen as so much of a virtue. Then patience is called for on the part of the Christians who are suffering—a much more difficult task for the faithful. Revelation 6:9-11 also shows that even the martyrs in heaven had a difficult time being patient. John said that God's patience was at an end. God was taking the decisive action that would assure the victory over evil and sin. Throughout the book, John called for patience, especially "patient endurance," until that decision of God, already begun in the heavenly realms, was carried out on earth.

The second consideration is that God has allowed evil some latitude because God created a humanity that could choose to be obedient. Throughout this book—and the entire Bible—there is a stress on obedience to God's will as something people can choose, once they know that will. The possibility of disobedience is therefore present. God did not desire puppets. And God therefore assumed the risk of sin and evil entering the world.

## The Beginning of the Victory

The victory over evil is not an easy matter. God does not simply reveal all the divine power and might with fierce clarity and overcome all enemies. The victory over evil is sufficiently gradual and hidden to allow choice. Even many who have succumbed to the power of evil may still choose God's side as the battle lines become more clearly drawn. This is implied in the quotation from Romans 2:4, above. God's patience is for the purpose of allowing repentance and change. Even the victory of God makes room for this. Evil within the world is destined to be gradually unmasked until, at last, it stands forth. The unmasking is a long process within human history, but when the final battle comes, evil will be seen clearly. Those whose lives are still under its allegiance will also be revealed for what they are.

In a certain sense, all of the Bible is the history of God's process of working against the evil powers. A people was chosen, beginning with Abraham. Gradually a nation was formed and trained to hear and understand God's word to it. The history of Israel, from Abraham through the return from the Exile, the books of the Law and the writings of the prophets, are all accounts of God's forming a people to be a light to the world—a beacon showing a sinful world God's desire and purpose for all of creation. Israel was not always faithful to this task. Its historians even recorded when she had been disobedient and what she had learned about God and herself in disobedience.

Finally the time came for a new and ultimate stage in this history of God's victory. The messianic community*—Israel—brought forth the One who was to be God's victor on earth. It is at this point that we can see the two-level character of the Book of Revelation and the somewhat confusing chronology that arises when we overlook the two-story structure. The vision of the throne of God in chapter four continues in chapter five. A scroll is in God's right hand, a scroll sealed with seven seals. The question is asked: Who is worthy to open the scroll? The answer resounds throughout the fifth chapter: "Worthy is the Lamb that was slain." This Lamb is further identified as "the Lion of the tribe of Judah, the Root of David." Clearly Jesus Christ, the crucified, risen, and ascended Lord is to open the seals.

Therefore, when these opening visions of the Book of Revelation are given, the scene in heaven shows that the victory of Christ has already been won. That victory was won, not in heaven but on earth. John, of course, knew this, for he was living more than a generation after these central events of the Christian faith.

And yet, chapter 12 is about the birth of the Messiah. Let us look at these strange verses.

## The Woman Clothed with the Sun

Chapter 12 introduces a woman of cosmic proportions! She is clothed with the sun, the moon is under her feet, and 12 stars form a crown for her head. She is about to have a child. This is a portent, or a sign, which here means a great wonder in the skies. It is almost as though this woman appears as a constellation in the heavens. She is obviously not a human figure—an individual woman of human history—although there may be connections between this heavenly figure and a specific woman. Many scholars believe that some Near Eastern myth lies behind this chapter, especially behind the figure of the woman clothed with the sun. That may be. From whatever sources, however, John's mind was filled with images which were used in the service of the visions that he had.

In the past centuries, especially in works of art, the Virgin Mary has often been pictured standing on the moon and with a crown of 12 stars on her head. The biblical passage itself makes clear that the woman is the mother of the Messiah. This does not refer directly to the historical mother Mary since the same woman is also described as bringing forth many other children, who are the rest of the faithful. The woman symbolizes the messianic community, the people of God formed so lovingly over so many centuries. The time has come for her to bring forth the One in whom God's victory will be won. And so the child is born of a woman from that messianic people. Throughout the Book of Revelation there is a constant stress on the connection between Israel and the Church.

Probably also in the mind of John was the ancient prophecy to be found in Genesis 3:15-16: the curses upon the serpent and upon Eve. At the point of the fall, God declared that the seed of the woman would bruise the head of the serpent and that the woman would have pain in childbirth. Here, in Revelation 12, both curses are apparent. The woman is pictured as being in pain and anguish. The child she bears is the One who is to conquer the serpent-dragon for all time. For this reason, also, the cosmic figure of the messianic people takes the form of a woman in travail.

The woman in 12:1 is the messianic community, Israel, whose time had come to bring forth the Messiah. The powers of evil, symbolized by the dragon, sought to kill the child as soon as it was born. The child was born, and God protected him. Finally, God took him up to the throne in heaven. It is not exactly clear what this means. If John had in mind a cosmic vision of the earthly history of Jesus, this refers to the Ascension. Some commentators have thought the chapter refers to a birth and enthronement of the Messiah in heaven before history.

At a point such as this, the two-level characteristic of the book makes it difficult if not impossible to be certain at what level this scene is to be understood. The same is true for the length of time, usually thought of as three and a half years, that the mother of the child is to be hidden and nurtured by God. The fact that there has been a reference to the historical community of Israel may make it more likely that the historical ascension of Christ is referred to here. It is to this that the Apostles' Creed points in the words, "He ascended into heaven and sitteth at the right hand of God."

Throughout his earthly life, Christ was pursued by the powers of evil. He was finally even put to death. It appeared that evil had conquered. Yet Christ was faithful unto death, and now he is exalted. On earth, a glimpse into his victory was given in the resurrection. In heaven, the fullness of his victory is seen.

## The Victory in Heaven

The magnitude of the victory becomes clear in Revelation 12:7-12. As soon as Christ ascends to the throne of God, a war breaks out in heaven between the Archangel Michael and his angels on one side and the dragon and its angels on the other.

There are several very important things to notice here. The victory of Christ precipitates the war in heaven. The decisive battle has been won by Christ on earth. Now, because of that, Michael and his angels are involved in a "clean-up" operation. It may be surprising to us that there was evil in heaven and that the devil, the great dragon, was actually in heaven. For Judaism and Christianity both, however, it is not possible to think of a devil who is independent of God. God created all things (Rev. 4:11). This has always been a central affirmation of the Jewish-Christian tradition. Therefore, the devil must have been part of the good creation of God. His being evil is due to his own rebellion, sometime after his good creation. This has been the way both Judaism and Christianity have dealt with the idea of the devil. He is a fallen angel.

That is the background of 12:7-12. But much more is implied here. That original rebellion was long ago. Heaven itself was infected by this turning from God. Now, because of the victory of Christ, heaven is cleansed of all such evil. Satan and his angels were finally cast out of heaven. But he was cast to earth. Therefore, the war in heaven caused two things to happen: heaven was freed of evil, and earth became the scene of even greater evil than before. Read again those strange words: "Rejoice then, O heaven and you that dwell therein! But woe to you, O earth and sea, for the devil has come down to you in great wrath, because he knows that his time is short!" (Rev. 12:12).[1]

Heaven knows the victory. Even the cosmic forces of evil have been conquered. Yet this means that evil is now going to be worse on the earth, the only sphere left to it. The demonic powers know that the battle is on. They are also aware that they are losing. So they struggle even harder than before.

At the end of chapter 12, the messianic community on earth, born of the same "mother" as the Messiah, is now pursued by the dragon. The dragon "makes

---

[1] There is an interesting parallel to this statement about the fall of Satan in Luke 10, where Jesus refers to Satan. When Jesus sends out the 70 disciples, he begins his journey from Galilee to Jerusalem. The disciples return, telling of their great success over the forces of evil. Jesus replies: "I saw Satan fall like lightning from heaven" (Luke 10:18). The victory is beginning even in the disciples' preaching in the name of Jesus, long before the cross, the resurrection, and the ascension. The imagery of the destruction of Satan's power in heaven is the same in Luke as in Revelation 12:9.

war on the rest of her offspring." For the Christians who were enduring increasing persecution, this highly symbolic picture drawn by John would clearly explain why their suffering was growing greater in spite of the victory over evil by Jesus Christ.

The victory really made matters worse than before, at least on earth. We are not accustomed to dealing with such peculiar victories! Evil, forced out of heaven, is concentrating all of its force on the earth, where the faithful must struggle against it. They therefore ought not to be surprised that the attacks against them are growing. In fact, they should expect a constant increase in the persecution against them.


## The Double Cause of Evil

According to John, the evil that has been let loose upon the earth in fuller measure than ever before has two sources:

1. the victory which has thrown to earth all of the evil power which had been in the heavenly realm.

2. the evil which is the consequence of sin.

Sin is not simply a matter of going against the will of God. It is this and more. God has created humanity and therefore knows very well how we are to live in order to be most fully human. To disobey these laws is not only to offend God but also to offend our own humanity. But our inhumanity also unleashes enormous evil upon the world. There are consequences of past evil actions that continue for generations, affecting even the lives of people who never know the cause of their present suffering. We can see such effects every time we read the newspapers: a dam breaks because of carelessness in its building or its inspection, and hundreds of people are killed. Someone is abused and traumatized as a child, and then, as a young adult, goes berserk and injures others, affecting many families who are total strangers.

Sin begets evil. Most of us have had first-hand knowledge of this. We discover that often we cannot take back what we have done, no matter how much we regret our actions. The consequences have gone too far. Multiplied millions of times, that is the situation in our world. We are living in the midst of the consequences of the sin of all generations past. Obviously the grace of God has also been active in our world, so many of the consequences of sin have been transformed by God's grace into blessings and new possibilities. The cross of Christ is the clearest and best example of this. The cross is the result of human sinfulness. Yet it is also the means by which God redeems us. Both statements are true, but only because the cross is an event in which God is active and bends sinful human deeds to God's purposes.

## God's Power Begins to Reign

From John's point of view, part of God's patience in the past has involved letting most of the consequences of sin have their dire results, thus causing great suffering. Now the time has come for God to judge and punish the evildoers in the world. No longer will sin be allowed to go on as before.[2] This means that the judgment of God is coming upon those who have perpetrated evil. For this reason also, things will be worse on the earth in the immediate future: the judgment of God is working itself out; Satan is cast from

---

[2] For this reason, we pray in the Lord's Prayer, "Thy will be done on earth as it is in heaven." Heaven is now totally under the sway of the will of God. Our prayer is that earth will be soon.

heaven to earth and the judgment of God upon the earth is increased at the same time. In some way, all these constitute the same event. Again, the faithful should not be surprised at the increase in suffering that is going to occur. Earth is being cleansed of evil through the judgment of God.

This element is stressed in the song of the 24 elders, already encountered as part of the heavenly host in 4:4. In 11:17-18 they sing:

*We give thanks to thee, Lord God Almighty, who art and who wast,*
*that thou hast taken thy great power and begun to reign.*
*The nations raged, but thy wrath came,*
*and the time . . .*
  *for destroying the destroyers of the earth.*

The judgment of God upon the earth results in increased suffering. Within this perspective the many visions of destruction in the Book of Revelation are to be put.

The victory of the Lamb really begins this whole process (Revelation 5). The Lamb that has conquered is Jesus, the Lamb that was slain. Because of his victory he is authorized to open the scroll sealed with the seven seals. As the seals are broken in heaven, the disasters begin on the earth. The first four seals let loose four horses and riders, generally referred to as the Four Horsemen of the Apocalypse. There have been various ways of identifying these horsemen; there is no total agreement. But the main point is clear: in their wake death, famine, war, pestilence are increased upon the earth. The other seals yield further disasters. The earth is terrified; everyone, from the rich to the poor, is hiding.

# The Wrath of the Lamb

According to 6:16-17, everyone is aware that the disasters are due to "the wrath of the Lamb." This does not mean that there is a personal vindictiveness on the part of Jesus, but rather that those who are evil feel this judgment upon them as wrath. We often quote the comforting verse, John 3:16. But we usually fail to go on to the rest of the passage that has a similar meaning to what is here called the wrath of the Lamb: "This is the judgment, that the light has come into the world, and [they] loved darkness rather than light, because their deeds were evil" (John 3:19).

There is a rigorousness here that may make us cringe. Surely God is a God of love, not a God of wrath! Surely Christ is more gentle and merciful than the picture we have of him in Revelation 19:11-16:

> Then I saw heaven opened, and behold, a white horse! He who sat upon it is called Faithful and True, and in righteousness he judges and makes war. His eyes are like a flame of fire, and on his head are many diadems; and he has a name inscribed which no one knows but himself. He is clad in a robe dipped in blood, and the name by which he is called is The Word of God. And the armies of heaven, arrayed in fine linen, white and pure, followed him on white horses. From his mouth issues a sharp sword with which to smite the nations, and he will rule them with a rod of iron; he will tread the wine press of the fury of the wrath of God the Almighty. On his robe and on his thigh he has a name inscribed, King of kings and Lord of lords.

There is a very difficult line that has to be drawn. On the one side, we must avoid placing God and Christ so much in the roles of judges that we wish to flee from their presence. We are not to seek ways, from a distance, to placate the anger and wrath that is due us because of our sin. As Martin Luther said, we cannot love a God from whom we wish to flee. On the other side, God does intend that the creation be the righteous, just, and good world it was created to be. There is an intolerance of evil built into God's dealing with us.

The Book of Revelation makes it clear that Christ is the one in whom God wins the victory over sin and evil within our world and our history. A vision is given of Christ who is going forth to conquer (19:11-16). The imagery of the wine press of God's wrath (19:13-15) picks up an ancient expression in Isaiah 63:1-6. In this passage God is pictured as saying: "I have trodden the wine press alone, and from the peoples no one was with me; I trod them in my anger and trampled them in my wrath; their lifeblood is sprinkled upon my garments, and I have stained all my raiment" (Isaiah 63:3).

These are indeed harsh visions. But they point to the truth that God will indeed conquer evil. There is forgiveness. Repentance is possible and often demanded in Revelation. If we continually side with evil, we shall find God and Christ against us.

Julia Ward Howe, in the early days of the American Civil War, wrote "The Battle Hymn of the Republic." The first stanza captures almost exactly the ideas of Revelation 19:11-16 in a similar visionary form:

*Mine eyes have seen the glory of the coming of the Lord;*
*He is trampling out the vintage where the grapes of wrath are stored;*
*He hath loosed the fateful lightning of his terrible swift sword;*
*His truth is marching on. (The United Methodist Hymnal)*

The following stanzas show the judgment implied for all of us and the role of Christ. Julia Ward Howe understood that God does permit evil and sin to run their course for a season. Yet when God determines that it shall end, woe be to those who choose to side with evil rather than with God.

## The Lull and the Final Battle

When we come to Revelation 20, we read one of the strangest and most controversial portions of this ancient writing. Let us review a moment where we are. A new and final victory over evil began in the cross, resurrection and ascension of Christ. This victory is now finished in heaven, but the battle has grown much worse on earth.

As chapter 20 opens, John's vision seems to include the total victory over evil on the earth. The powers of evil are chained and cast into the lake of fire. This victory is only to last a thousand years. Then Satan is to be released again and the final battle will take place. This thousand year period of relative peace is often called the millenium.*

Especially within the United States there has been enormous interest in this passage. In the past century and a half, new churches have begun because of different interpretations of these verses. These groups can be divided roughly into pre-millenialists* and post-millenialists.* The debate has to do with whether or not the return of Christ is at the beginning or end of the thousand year period. Obviously, it is difficult to base an entire view of history on a few verses of scripture whose message is not totally clear, as is the case of Revelation 20. But this has been the temptation, especially for groups in our society who feel powerless, either because of poverty or because of changes taking place so rapidly that they feel helpless.

The passage itself is confusing or, at least, ambiguous. Are the dead who are raised in the first resurrection here on the earth or in heaven? Are the nations who form "Gog and Magog," the enemies of the saints, present but inactive during the thousand years? Answers to these sorts of questions have given rise to various millenial schemes.

What did all of this mean to those to whom John wrote? It is clear that in verses 20:4-6 there is a promise of triumph for those who suffer because of Christ. This is a call to steadfastness. But what of the rest of the passage? One thing is certain. John was aware that evil forces are not to be quickly and easily subdued forever. The evil powers are chained "for a thousand years." Why then are they let loose again? Evidently to give a final choice for the inhabitants of the earth. A final testing takes place. John is abrupt in his vision of the conclusion of this last struggle: the forces of evil mobilize, but no battle really takes place. Fire comes down from heaven, and they are all destroyed.

## The Judgment

After this comes the judgment of all who have lived. This is similar to the scene of judgment in Matthew 25:31-46. It is also reminiscent of what we have already discussed concerning "the wrath of the Lamb." God is very much concerned with our actions.

Evidently faithfulness to Christ leads us to know accurately what is good to do and to choose it. Lack of faithfulness can lead us to do evil, for we can be easily deceived into believing it is good or, at least, acceptable to commit evil deeds. Evil seduces us into thinking that it is all right. Vigilance is required so that we are not deceived. The letters to the seven churches are filled with warnings that some of the congregations had lost their earlier ability to choose the good and had compromised their consciences. Compromise is relatively easy when the society around us assures us that it is acceptable to do what everyone else is doing. The church has a difficult time going against such public opinion and maintaining the clarity of its own views of good and evil. The final judgment will show clearly who has compromised and who has not.

This emphasis on remaining faithful to Christ and not compromising with evil is the heart of John's message to the churches. Although put in the context of great cosmic imagery, the message is quite simple. Those who remain faithful will be victorious. Those who are not faithful will never gain the peace that is final and lasting. Such a vision of the ultimate future adds great significance to the decisions Christians are called on to make every day. It warns them not to assume that their decisions are trivial and do not really matter to God. That is a message Christians in every generation need to hear.

# Studying This Chapter

## Purpose of the Chapter

It is easy to get lost in the symbolism of the Book of Revelation and to lose sight of the overall purpose of John's vision. The main purpose in this third chapter is to call attention to the centrality of Christ in the plan of God in the Book of Revelation. Christ's role in God's victory over evil is especially important.

## Questions and Suggested Methods

1) This chapter deals with the peculiar victory of Christ which makes life worse upon the earth than it was before his victory. This is a very difficult idea to grasp. One of the parallel situations we often encounter in our own lives is "backlash." When a cause most Christians agree is good and just begins to

gain strength and win victories, then the attacks upon it increase enormously. At that point, many of us decide to give up struggling since our efforts seem to produce greater evil. Ask the class to describe similar situations in which they have been involved or about which they have read. How would the Book of Revelation help them to interpret these events? Would it give them guidance on how to be faithful Christians in these times?

2) Especially if we are in fairly comfortable situations, we may think that the disasters mentioned in Revelation only occur elsewhere in the world. It becomes easy to say that we are safe from these disasters because God loves us and does not cause those he loves to suffer. What does Revelation say?

3) Call on those who were chosen as reporters to share their discoveries with the class. This might best be done after the class has begun to discuss that section of the study, so that the class does not spend all its time comparing other peoples' views. Try to stimulate some real struggle with the passages by the class itself, using commentaries as aids.

4) Ask the class to describe the temptations to compromise that Christians in our own country face. Then, on the basis of that list, have the class draw up a description of someone totally faithful to Christ, someone who does not compromise at all, in our own time. Finally, ask the class to list the things that keep us from fulfilling that description in our own lives.

## Preparing for the Next Study

The next study will deal with the evil which has been let loose upon the earth, particularly with the interconnection of all evil.

To get ready for that study it may be useful to ask several members of the group to prepare very brief reports on some of the evils and problems which are present in today's world. Assign a particular topic to each person—world hunger, the ecological crisis, crime in the cities, corporations paying bribes to governments, drug traffic, etc. Ask each person to be ready to give a brief report, no more than two minutes, on the subject assigned.

It may also be helpful to collect current newspaper clippings dealing with these issues and to put them up on a wall or on tables. When the group is discussing the Book of Revelation, it therefore will understand that it is dealing with real evil and not with something of the past, or something that exists only in the mind.

# 4
# The Power of Evil

*Revelation 13—18*

In the last chapter we studied the victory of the Lamb. Now we will turn our attention to the nature of the conflict and, more particularly, to the power of evil. How does Revelation describe the evil powers against which Christians are to struggle and over which the Lamb has won the victory?

## The Trilogies of Evil

In Revelation 12 Satan is described as a red or, more literally, a fiery dragon "with seven heads and ten horns, and seven diadems upon his heads" (12:3). This dragon tried to devour the son of the woman clothed with the sun. But God had other plans, for this son of the messianic community was "to rule all the nations with a rod of iron," and was therefore "caught up to God and to his throne" (12:4-5). Thereafter a heavenly battle ensued, with the result that the dragon was cast out of heaven and is now upon the earth (12:9-10). This is a joyful event for heaven, but a woeful event for earth and sea (12:12). Because of this heavenly battle, evil has increased on earth.

Underlying all evil is the primordial[1] evil repre-

[1] **primordial:** fundamental, original, source.

sented by the dragon (Satan or the serpent). Therefore, although there are references to concrete incarnations of evil in Revelation, all these are to be placed within the context of the fact that Satan, having been conquered in heaven, is now making his last stand on earth.

As we begin reading chapter 13, we receive the impression that the "beast rising out of the sea" is the dragon. This beast, too, has seven heads and ten horns—although this beast wears its diadems, not upon its heads, as did the dragon, but upon its horns. The beast is not really the dragon itself but rather an agent of its will (13:4). The symbolism of the seven heads and ten horns of the beast is partially explained in 17:9-16, to which we shall turn at the appropriate time.

A second beast appears. In 13:11 we read about "another beast which rose out of the earth." This beast has two horns like a lamb but speaks like a dragon. This description of the second beast reveals the way John understood the power of evil. His purpose, when speaking of a certain number of heads, or horns, or the like was not to make the power of evil appear fearsome. It was to show that, to the unwary, they may look like the power of good. This second beast appears to be a lamb, but, in reality, its speech comes from the dragon. The same is true of the seven heads and ten horns belonging to both the dragon and the sea-beast.

Both seven and ten were considered to be numbers* signifying wholeness, perfection. The Lamb has seven horns and seven eyes (5:6). The purpose of this is not to depict Christ as a nightmarish creature but to show the perfection of his power and wisdom. Likewise, when we are told that the dragon has seven heads, the purpose is not to describe him as a repulsive being, like those we see in monster movies. It is to show he seems to be good and wholesome. The same is true of the beast from the sea.

In any case, what we have is a trilogy of evil: the dragon (identified elsewhere as Satan or the serpent), the beast from the sea and the beast from the earth. Later on, the list varies somewhat, for there is the dragon, the beast, and the "false prophet" (Rev. 16:13). Still further on, there is a great harlot, who sits upon a red beast which has seven heads and ten horns (Rev. 17). Presumably, this is a new image, where the harlot takes the place of the beast from the earth and of the false prophet. Thus, we could list the trilogy of evil in at least three different ways:

| The Trilogies of Evil | | |
|---|---|---|
| **I** | **II** | **III** |
| **1.** the dragon | the dragon | the dragon |
| **2.** the beast from the sea | the beast | the beast |
| **3.** the beast from the earth | the false prophet | the great harlot |

There is a great deal in these trilogies which is difficult to understand. To this day, scholars are divided as to the exact meaning of different symbols, images and numbers connected with the various members of these trilogies. We shall return to some of these issues later on. But first, it may be well to point out some of the elements that are clear from these trilogies.

The first trilogy makes it clear that the problem of evil is not necessarily limited to one sphere of creation. Some might think that evil is earthly in nature, that somehow it has to do with the fact that things on earth, including our bodies, are physical. At the time when John had his visions, there were Christians who blamed their material bodies for the evil in them and the matter out of which earth is made for the evil in it. But the Book of Revelation is very clear. The dragon is a heavenly being. There is a beast that arises out of the sea. And there is another that comes from the earth. Thus, neither earth, nor sea, nor even heaven, is totally free from evil—at least not until the most recent times, when Satan was finally cast out of heaven.

Secondly, every trilogy is headed by the dragon, Satan himself. This means that, whatever concrete forms evil might take in the third element of the trilogies, we are dealing not merely with some particularly bad government or religion but *Evil* itself, with a capital E. There are probable concrete interpretations of the third element in some of these trilogies. But whatever those concrete evils may be, John was dealing with *Evil*—symbolized by the dragon, Satan, or the primeval serpent.

Finally, the second element in all three trilogies is also constant. The beast from the sea cannot be identified with primordial *Evil,* since it receives its authority from the dragon. Yet, it appears at the root of all the concrete manifestations of *Evil*, as depicted by the third member of the various trilogies. Who or what is this beast that seems to pervade John's vision of evil?

## The Beast from the Sea

John's vision of the beast from the sea is reminiscent of the vision of the four beasts which appears in Daniel 7. There, the prophet saw four different beasts coming out of the sea. The first was like a winged lion, the second like a bear, the third like a leopard with four wings and four heads and the fourth was a terrible beast with iron teeth and ten horns. John combined in a single beast the features of Daniel's four beasts: "the beast that I saw was like a *leopard*, its feet were like a *bear*'s, and its mouth was like a *lion*'s mouth. And to it the *dragon* gave his power and his throne and great authority" (Rev. 13:12).

The vision in Daniel can be explained entirely in terms of political history: the various beasts and horns are just as many kings or kingdoms, whereas the same cannot be said of John's vision. In Revelation 17:9-17 there is an explanation of the heads and horns of the beast in terms of political history. But in Revelation 12:3 the seven heads and ten horns are attributed to the dragon, who is a heavenly being which existed prior to the kings discussed in chapter 17. The seven heads and ten horns of the dragon and of the beast, as well as the seven diadems of the dragon and the beast's ten, are not symbols for actual kings, kingdoms or political events. Rather, the numbers seven and ten denote perfection, completion, and thus indicate the beast's—and the dragon's—complete evil. In John's beast from the sea, all evil has rallied into one great power. The four beasts of Daniel have joined in one.

Another baffling element in John's description of the beast from the sea is his assertion that "one of its heads seemed to have a mortal wound, but its mortal wound was healed, and the whole earth followed the beast with wonder" (Rev. 13:3). This confusing allusion can be joined with two similar sayings in 17:8: "The beast that you saw was, and is not, and is to ascend from the bottomless pit and go to perdition," and "behold the beast, because it was and is not and is to come." Puzzling over the possible meanings of these phrases, some interpreters have pointed to the legend of the return of Nero, which was relatively popular in the Roman Empire after Nero's death. In its original form, the legend claimed that Nero had not really killed himself but had escaped to Persia, where he was preparing an army with which to invade the empire. This notion may have been fostered by some of the authorities who wished to increase the motivation of the masses and the soldiers in their repeated wars with Persia. In any case, the legend eventually developed to claim that Nero had, in fact, died but would rise again in the east to attack the empire. According to some interpretations, the wounded head that was healed is an allusion to Nero and to this legend.

There is no doubt that John knew of the fear which the Roman Empire felt towards its Persian neighbors. This can be seen in Revelation 16:12, where one of the plagues which God unleashes is to dry up the Euphrates, "to prepare the way for the kings from the east." But here any eastern invasion is the work of God, not of the beast or of one of its heads.

It seems much simpler and accurate to relate the seemingly cryptic sayings of Revelation 13:3 and 17:8 to the experience of John and of those to whom he wrote. The message of the Gospel—indeed, John's message too—is that in Christ the power of evil has been defeated. This was a mortal blow inflicted upon the head of the beast. And yet, as the daily experience of Christians continuously demonstrates, the beast is still alive. There are persecutions and all the evils mentioned in the letters to the seven churches. The beast, although in a sense killed by Christ, is still alive. Or, using the imagery of the previous study, the victory that has taken place in heaven is hardly visible on earth. Thus, although the beast is fatally wounded, it is still alive.

The references in 17:8 are easily explained in the same manner. The beast was and is not because Christ has defeated it. But, that victory is not yet final. The beast still roams the earth and makes its power felt; in fact, its power will seem to become even stronger before its final defeat.

## The Beast from the Sea
## and the Beast from the Earth

In Revelation 13, after describing his vision of the beast from the sea, John describes a second beast "which rose out of the earth." This beast has the power to lead people astray and to make them worship the beast from the sea. Its power is similar to that of the prophets of old for it can even make "fire come down from heaven." Thus, the second trilogy probably refers to this beast when it speaks of "the false prophet" (16:13).

This beast has the power to organize human society in such a way that all will serve evil. Without bearing its mark, people cannot perform normal functions such as buying or selling. This is true of the rich as well as the poor, of the slave as well as the free (Rev. 13:16-17).

Exactly what that mark is, John never tells us. He simply says that in order to form part of normal society all will have to have either the name or the number of the beast on their right hand or on their forehead. The number is 666. For centuries different interpreters have tried to find some mysterious meaning in the number of the beast. This has become particularly prevalent in recent times when means have been found to apply this seemingly mysterious number to anyone who happens to be the interpreter's arch-enemy. Thus at various times different people have applied the number of the beast (always with seeming good reason) to the Pope, Luther, Hitler, Stalin, Richard Nixon, Germany, Japan, Russia and a host of others.

There is a basic flaw in all these interpretations. Not only is the Book of Revelation the word of God for us. It was also the word of God for John's contemporaries, as well as for Christians in the tenth century or the sixteenth century. If, as some claim, the Book of Revelation refers in detail to the events of our day and not to any others, how was it the word of God for those other Christians of earlier centuries? Was it intended to remain for them an absolutely closed book simply because they did not know of Hitler, or Stalin, or whomever? Was the message to them simply that here were some mysteries which did not make much sense but which would eventually come true? Was John really writing to the churches in Asia, or was he not? If he was, could they not understand his message until some "enlightened" 20th-century interpreter came along? Put in another way, John may have been referring concretely to the conditions in Asia in his time or he may have been speaking in more general terms. In either case, the revelation which he recorded can still be God's word to us, just as the rest of the Bible is, and show us the nature of God's dealings with humankind. But if John was writing concretely about *our* time, practically with names and addresses as some claim, how were his words the word of God to the churches in Asia?

In any case, there is a relatively simple explanation of the number 666 proposed by some scholars. This explanation was recorded by Irenaeus of Lyon, who claimed that his teacher Polycarp was himself a disciple of John! Irenaeus knew the Book of Revelation well. His writings show not only that he had read it but that he shared in much of its spirit. About the number 666, Irenaeus simply said that it is the epitome of all rebellion against God. Just as the number seven is the sign of perfection, the number six is the opposite. Here we have *six* hundreds, *six* tens and *six* units. In spite of all its posing as divine, the beast has a "human number" (Rev. 13:18), a number of imperfection—666!

Finally, the strength of the beast from the earth is neither that of a foreign power nor that of a coercive dictatorship. The beast convinces people by means of its great marvels and then controls society in such a way that people kill those who refuse to worship it. Only by becoming one of its servants can people buy or sell—that is, be a part of organized society. John is speaking not of an unpopular regime but quite the opposite! It is an orderly society which requires that its members partake of common idolatry. Most of its members do not seem to feel oppressed by such conditions.

## The Beast and the Great Harlot

In Revelation 17, one of the seven angels with the cups of wrath shows John "the judgment of the great harlot who is seated upon many waters" (17:1). John is transported "in the Spirit" into a wilderness. There he sees a woman seated upon a beast whose description is the same as that of the beast from the sea in Revelation 13:1. This woman is decked in all sorts of finery, but in her hand she holds "a golden cup full of abominations and the impurities of her fornication" (17:4). Also, she is "drunk . . . with the blood of the martyrs of Jesus" (17:6). On her forehead is written "a name of mystery," which says "Babylon the great, mother of harlots and of earth's abominations" (17:5).

The "great harlot" is Rome. Almost all scholars agree on this point. She "is the great city which has dominion over the kings of the earth" (17:18), and sits on "seven hills" (17:9), which is one of the classical ways of referring to Rome. The name, "Babylon," is also a fairly common way in which Jews and Christians have referred in various times to the political powers that have persecuted them. Also, this great harlot has been drinking the blood of the martyrs, and has been committing "fornication"—a common biblical symbol for idolatry. Terrible woes await this new Babylon.

The meaning of the "great harlot" is fairly clear; but the symbolism related to the beast is quite confusing and has baffled interpreters for generations. The beast is described in terms similar to the beast from the sea. Yet here the seven heads and ten horns seem to be given an interpretation in terms of political history. The seven heads are at once the seven hills on which the harlot sits and seven kings, "five of whom have fallen, one is, the other has not yet come" (17:10). This has puzzled exegetes[2] who have tried to relate what is known of the succession of Roman emperors with this description. They have suggested many different solutions, none of which is entirely satisfactory. This failure has encouraged more popular interpreters to try to relate these seven kings to various events in our time, just as they have attempted to uncover the meaning of the number 666.

As in the case of the number of the beast, we would do well to remember the meaning of the numbers six and seven for John. Seven denotes perfection; six is the opposite. The woes of the sixth seal (6:12-17) and of the sixth trumpet (9:13-21) are the greatest of all signs of the impending end. The number six, then, in a series of seven denotes the moment of decision—just as we speak of "the eleventh hour" in our sequence of twelve. Thus, the "seven kings" are not necessarily to be equated with seven actual rulers, but refer to the fact that most of history is past (five kings) and that the hour of decision has arrived. This is why when the seventh comes "he must remain only a little while" (17:10): his very coming will be the completion.

The interpretation of the ten horns is fascinating (17:12-17). They represent "ten kings" (again, a number denoting fullness) who will fight against both Christ the Lamb (17:14) and Rome the harlot (17:16). Thus, the enemies of God are used to destroy other enemies. But John did not believe that the destruction of the harlot would put an end to evil. When the harlot is gone, the beast will still be powerful (17:17). John did not make the common error of identifying *Evil* completely with its manifestations, thinking that once a manifestation was destroyed *Evil* would be overcome.

## Evil in God's Hands

The fact that the ten kings who war against Christ are also the ones who will devour the flesh of the harlot is an example of an element in the Book of Revelation which we must not forget: God uses what seems to be evil in order to carry forth the divine purpose (Rev. 15, 16, and 18). We are told of seven angels with "seven golden bowls full of the wrath of God" (15:7). These angels go out and pour their bowls upon the earth. At the first bowl "foul and evil sores" come upon those who bear "the mark of the beast and worshipped its image" (16:2). Remember, these are

[2]**exegete:** one who interprets and explains scripture or other writings.

the "decent folk" who share in the normal life of the community, the only ones who can "buy and sell" (13:17). The second bowl kills every living creature in the sea; the third turns the rivers to blood; the fourth makes the sun so hot that people burn; the fifth is poured on the very throne of the beast; the sixth dries up the Euphrates "to prepare the way for the kings from the east" (16:12) to invade the empire; and, finally, the seventh produces such destruction that every island and mountain disappear (16:20). A similar picture appears in chapter 18, where the fall of Babylon (Rome) is described. Economic disruption is caused by that fall (18:11-19), over which heaven, saints, apostles and prophets rejoice (18:20).

We must be careful not to equate evil with what is uncomfortable or destroys our securities. The message of these sections of the Book of Revelation is that the powers of evil try to persuade us that they are good. The powers appear with seven heads, and claim to be perfect; or they make themselves up to look like the Lamb, but their speech is the dragon's. The beast from the earth performs miracles to induce people to worship the beast from the sea. Furthermore, the beast from the earth manages to organize society in such a fashion that any who refuse to bear its mark, to compromise, will be excluded from all normal social transactions. In the midst of this situation, Christians are called upon to do two things. The first is not to compromise. The Book of Revelation is very clear about that. The second is to know that a great deal of what seems to be evil, according to the beast's social order, may be God's wrath upon Babylon and may therefore be good. The Book of Revelation is even clearer about this second point.

A proper interpretation of the Book of Revelation for our time, therefore, will not seek simply to set our

minds at ease about the evils and the woes
rampant in the world. There is indeed a note
dence and joy in the Book of Revelation—
strong note. But it is a note that sounds ou
awful cacophony of real pain, woe and evil.
tory of the Lamb comes through suffering ev
death. The final victory comes through the
out of the bowls of God's wrath. The Book of Revelation does not teach Christians to live in a fairyland
fantasy of happy endings and mellow conflicts.
Rather, it encourages Christians to live in the harsh
world in which evil is making its last stand and to face
that evil with no illusions about its remaining strength.

Finally, a proper interpretation of the Book of Revelation will help us distinguish between God's good
purposes and the "goods" which our own civilization
constantly tries to peddle to us. The Book of Revelation does not promise that our world order will sur-
vive but that God's order will be established. It is
difficult but important to learn to distinguish between
these two.

# Studying This Chapter

## Purpose of the Chapter

The purpose of this chapter is to show that in the
Book of Revelation good and evil are seen in a wide
perspective, so that things which appear good may be
evil, and vice versa. This means that Christians cannot
simply accept what society tells them about good and
evil. They must judge such matters on the basis of
their knowledge of God's eternal purposes of love and

justice. Hopefully, the group will also discover the interconnection of evil. Some of the things which they consider good may be deeply related to great evils. One example is North American affluence and its relationship to world hunger.

## Questions and Suggested Methods

1) Place around the room newspaper clippings about the various woes which confront the world today. As people arrive, make sure they read these and that the conversation revolves around them. This will set the mood for the study.

2) Ask those who have prepared them to present their brief reports on these issues.

3) Lead a discussion about the relationship among these various items. In the discussion try to avoid two pitfalls. The first is talking about each item separately. The discussion is not about them but about the themes that bind them together—relate them to each other. The second pitfall is to jump too quickly to the relatively easy answer "sin." It is true that sin lies at the root of all evil. But the Book of Revelation encourages us to look also at the intermediate element, at the forms which sin takes in our day.

4) Then move to the question, "What does the Book of Revelation, particularly the chapters we are studying today, tell us about how we are to view these problems which we confront?" For this discussion you may wish to concentrate on some concrete issues, such as the ecological crisis or crime in our cities.

## Preparing for the Next Study

We have seen that the victory over evil has indeed been won, and yet, we have also seen the pervasive and frightful character of evil that remains within our world. In our next chapter we shall focus on how John's vision portrays the life of the faithful in the midst of all this evil. How do their lives differ from lives without faith?

One of the chief emphases for next time will be the place of prayer and baptism in the Christian life. Ask the group to keep a list, mental or written, of occasions when they have heard or read something about the meaning of baptism. This may be in a sermon, a hymn, a church publication, etc. These will then be shared in the next meeting as part of a discussion question.

Also, if the discussions of problems in this study have mentioned local situations, keep a list of these for next time. Keep any reports or clippings that were used concerning them for the next meeting.

# 5
# The Calling
# of the Faithful

*Revelation 7:1—11:14; 19:1-10*

The victory has been accomplished by Christ, yet the power of evil is strong upon the earth. The faithful know both of these truths. How then ought they to live now, in the midst of such victory and such evil? The Book of Revelation is, in the last analysis, extremely practical. In spite of all the visions that may be confusing, the goal of Revelation is to aid Christians in deciding how to live their lives.

In our last two studies, we learned that John's visions widen the context within which Christians live their lives. That is to say, those who heard John's message could no longer think that the little decisions they had to make about local matters were unimportant in the divine scheme of things. Local problems are part of the larger fabric of evil that envelops the whole earth. The Christian's refusal to compromise with evil in its local forms is the refusal to wear the sign of the beast. It is a significant matter. It is the decision to be a faithful witness to Jesus Christ and to the victory that Christians know by faith he has won.

# The 144,000

John began the seventh chapter with a description of the faithful 144,000: twelve thousand from each of the twelve tribes of Israel. These may represent Jews or Jewish-Christians. John was apparently closely tied to the Jewish-Christian community. There is no general agreement among scholars concerning whether the 144,000 of 7:4-8 are the same as the countless host of 7:9. They seem to be different groups, the first composed of a specific number of Jews and the second of a countless number of non-Jews. What makes interpretation difficult is the church's frequent use of the term "Israel" to apply to itself and the fact that 144,000 is a round number, twelve times twelve thousand. This number signifies the fullness of Israel. There are many instances of this number in Revelation, especially in the description of the new Jerusalem. Twelve gates are named for the 12 tribes of Israel and 12 foundations for the 12 apostles of the new Israel (Rev. 21). Even the 24 elders that surround the throne of God may represent 12 from the original Israel and 12 from the new.

Therefore, here at the beginning of the seventh chapter of Revelation, something is said about both the old and the new Israel. Both are part of the final people of God. The promise of God to Abraham and to his descendants has indeed been kept. And beyond Israel there is the expansion of the promise to those of every nation, race, tribe, and language. All of this points to the universal and inclusive character of the Church.

The number 144,000 is mentioned again in Revelation 14:1-4. The 144,000 "have not defiled themselves with women, for they are virgins" (14:4). These are very strange words which have caused scholars to raise many questions about the verse. Some believe it is a later textual addition by someone who wanted to show that monks were the highest form of church life. However, there is no evidence in the early manuscripts of any alternative reading here.

There is a much simpler explanation. The Old Testament frequently uses the imagery of fornication or adultery to stand for idolatry of the people against God. Those who are virgins are then those who have not been idolatrous and have refused to worship the beast. Here, in Revelation 14:4, the image is of men who have not been defiled with women. This also occurs in the Old Testament when the prophets speak against the practice of men in Israel participating with sacred prostitutes in the fertility cults of Canaan. The imagery of chaste men is apt in John's vision since in chapter 17 evil is going to be characterized as a harlot or prostitute. Therefore, 14:4 probably refers to those who have kept themselves pure from involvement with the evil of the beast incarnated in the great harlot.

Most women in our day—and probably in the past as well—resent having women in general cast as temptresses and as symbols for evil and idolatry. This has been done for centuries, as in this passage. In the Bible, however, the figures of women are used symbolically not only for evil but also for good. This is particularly true in Revelation. The woman clothed with the sun, the figure of the messianic community which brings forth both the Messiah and the faithful who are the brothers and sisters of the Messiah, is one positive symbol. There is one other similar image— the final community of faith, the new Jerusalem, is called the Bride of Christ (19:6-9; 21:1-9).

Revelation 14:4 also makes clear that the 144,000 are not the only people who are redeemed. Rather they are the first fruits, the sign that the full harvest is occurring.

## The Sealing of the Faithful

The 144,000 are "sealed" between the opening of the sixth and seventh seals of the scroll (7:3-4). The sealing of the 144,000 is to be a protection for them in the great tribulation that the trumpets of the angels announce. But what does "sealing" mean? In our day-to-day life, we are used to the term "seal" referring to closing something securely. We seal envelopes and canned goods. Sealing is a way of preserving privacy and keeping things from contamination. Sealing as a way of keeping something closed is the meaning of seal in the description of the scroll that was sealed with seven seals (Rev. 5:1). Something quite different is meant by sealing in 7:3-4. Sealing is a mark made to show to whom something or someone belongs. It is more like a brand made with a branding iron. The term seal is used for both the seals on the scroll and the sealing of the 144,000 because in ancient cultures the metal seal of the king was used both to seal documents with wax or lacquer and to make an identification mark. The 144,000 are marked to show that they belong to God (see also Ezekiel 9:4). With this sign they will be able to withstand the powers of evil that surround them and are about to become worse in the world.

Seal also has a liturgical or worship meaning that John's readers would have known. Very early in the church's life, the term "seal" began to be used for baptism. John's first readers would have understood that similarities to Christian baptism are to be found throughout this passage. This is not to say that the sealing of the 144,000 simply means that they were baptized. Rather it means that in this vision of the marking of the 144,000, Christians recognized overtones of what had happened to themselves in baptism. In fact, the mark of the beast would have been seen as the opposite of baptism.

For the early church, baptism implied more than it usually does for us today. It was entrance into the people of God. But it was also the actual imparting of a royal and priestly character to all of those baptized. Baptism was usually followed by an anointing with oil, which was the ancient sign in Israel of both the high priest and the king. There are echoes of this in Revelation 5:9-10, where the faithful are described as "from every tribe and tongue and people and nation" and are called "a kingdom and priests to our God." This same thought is found in I Peter 2:9-10. The priestly and kingly power that the baptized possess was directly related to the victory won by Christ. His power over the forces of evil was shared with them in baptism, so that they too would be able to conquer.

The early church often referred to baptism as "illumination" since through it Christians could come to an accurate knowledge of good and evil and not be taken in by the deceits of the beast.

Baptism was also a joining in the death and resurrection of Christ. In ways that we can scarcely imagine, the early church understood a connection between baptism and death. Paul had written: "You have died, and your life is hid with Christ in God" (Col. 3:3) and "You were buried with [Christ] in baptism" (Col. 2:12). Baptism was a seal that an individual had already begun to die to the old life. In a situation where persecution was a real threat, this dying to the old life could become concrete and immediate in martyrdom. In fact, martyrdom was visibly living out as a witness to the world the full meaning of Christian baptism. Martyrdom soon came to be called a "baptism by blood." In the vision of the countless multitude before the throne, the righteous are wearing white robes (Rev. 7:9-17). This refers to the baptismal robes that were used in the early church. These robes of the heavenly multitude had been made white by being washed in the blood of the Lamb. The people themselves had come through "the great tribulation." They were promised relief from their past sufferings: "They shall hunger no more, neither thirst any more; the sun shall not strike them, nor any scorching heat . . . and God will wipe away every tear from their eyes" (7:16, 17).

The 144,000 were sealed, not to protect them from harm but to enable them to remain faithful to Christ and to become martyrs. What a strange kind of protection this seems to be! Surely we would hope for protection that would keep us from suffering. John's vision offered no such guarantee. Most of the compromises with evil that John was attacking were caused by a desire to maintain physical and emotional comfort and to avoid suffering. That is probably still true for us today. We are always tempted to think that our comfort is a sign of God's blessing and to avoid the costly discipleship that could lead to suffering and pain. The Book of Revelation challenges these notions. The 144,000 were considered fortunate, they were promised strength to avoid compromises. For this reason, they would become martyrs. In the midst of conflict with evil, they would be victorious.

## The Victory of the Faithful

Our concept of victory over evil probably includes the idea that evil will lessen or cease and everything will be better. That is not what is meant by the victory of the faithful in the Book of Revelation (see especially the letters to the seven churches). Their victory is not that they have destroyed the evil powers that oppose them. Christ has done that, although that victory is still hidden on the earth. Rather, the victory of the faithful is that they have *remained* faithful, even though faithfulness seems foolish and futile to the non-believers. John held that the one who is faithful has conquered, even though nothing appears to have been altered. For this reason, martyrdom is such a great victory; also for this reason, compromise is so tempting.

In our own pragmatic culture we have a difficult time seeing martyrdom as a victory. Unless evil is lessened by our actions and the situation is changed for the better, we assume it is useless to act. This means that the greatest battle is always within ourselves. If we are faithful regardless of the cost, then we have been victorious. If we are not faithful, we cannot use the excuse that it would not have done any good anyway. It is not our task to win the victory over evil. It has already been won by Christ. Our faithfulness is to live as witnesses to the victory already won. Sometimes our faithfulness may bring changes for the better in the world. Sometimes it may even make matters worse, even as life for Christians became worse in the world after the victory of Christ.

Surely the Christians who received this letter would have been reminded of the claim made upon them by their own baptism. They would have been reminded—even as we need constantly to be reminded—that our baptism offers no guarantee of safe and secure existence. But it does offer the promise of God's presence and strength to be faithful in spite of suffering and persecution. This strength is ours whenever we turn in faith to God, willing to live out of the truth that in Christ, God has conquered sin, evil, and even death itself.

## Prayer as an Act of Faithfulness

How can we, in the midst of our struggles to be faithful here on earth, gain access to that strength God provides? The Book of Revelation gives us a clue: in 5:8 we read that the 24 elders had "golden bowls full of incense, which are the prayers of the saints." And in 8:3-4: "Another angel . . . was given much incense to mingle with the prayers of all the saints upon the golden altar before the throne; and the smoke of the incense rose with the prayers of the saints from the hand of the angel before God." We are given a glimpse of the reception in heaven of the prayers of the faithful. These are not bland prayers but an outcry for justice and judgment. We are assured that such prayers are not only heard but that they call forth the activity of heaven on our behalf.

This vision would not have been as unfamiliar to John's original readers as it probably is to us. For most of us, angels are not a major feature in our religious life, nor are incense and golden altars part of our usual worship experience. John's vision here was of a heavenly temple that was, in many ways, the counterpart of the earthly temple that had stood in Jerusalem until A.D. 70. This temple had been the center of Jewish religious life. For Jews who did not live in Jerusalem, the prayers of each evening were thought of as similar to—and even as a substitute for—the temple service, as we see in Psalm 141:2: "Let my prayer be counted as incense before thee, and the lifting up of my hands as an evening sacrifice." Within Judaism, prayer was connected with incense. As the incense rose to heaven, so did the prayers of the faithful, purified also by their contact with the incense. For Judaism before the time of John, there was also a widespread belief that angels, with proper names frequently given to them, had the task of carrying the prayers of the faithful to the throne of God. Many Christians have continued using the names of these angels, such as Michael, Gabriel and Raphael.

The model of prayer for the Christians of John's day was the model we still use: the Lord's Prayer. We have already seen how the phrase, "thy will be done on earth as it is in heaven," would have added meaning in the context of John's vision. Heaven had been cleansed through the victory of Christ. The church's fervent prayer was that the earth also would soon become a sphere in which there would be no opposition to the will of God. With all of the pressure Christians felt to compromise their faithfulness, the words, "Lead us not into temptation but deliver us from evil," would have had more meaning for them than for most of us. Within the context of Revelation, this would be a petition to keep us from the power of the beast and the dragon. Only when we are aware of the possibility of compromise and the cost of obedience, do we feel we must turn to God for strength against temptation.

When the times are not as obviously dangerous for Christians as they were in the first century, when it appears that no great idolatries are tempting us to turn aside from the path of faith, then prayer does not seem as much a necessity. In seemingly easy situations, prayer may lose its centrality in the life of faith. But, as in the letter to the church at Laodicea, such a sense of security may be our downfall.

For many of us, prayer is a duty, and perhaps we feel guilty if we do not pray. Often we speak of prayer as a privilege for Christians. Surely it is that. Yet the term privilege makes it sound like an option we may or may not use as we see fit. For Christians in the midst of persecution, prayer is a matter of life and death. When tempted to compromise, prayer becomes a means of gaining strength. John's vision was an assurance that these prayers would be effective. In a sense, prayer allows the Christian, still in the midst of the conflict with evil in this world, to be present at the victory of the Lamb in heaven, for the prayers are received there. This is poetic imagery, but it points to the truth that those who turn to prayer in order to remain faithful are given a share in the victory which Christ has already won. For this reason, the experience of prayer is also the experience of gaining power to stand firm.

## The Task of the Faithful Prophet

In chapters ten and eleven, John paints a picture of the difficult role of the prophet in the times that lay ahead. He himself is the first prophet he considered. We have already discussed his place as a prophet in the church in Asia. But also, in his vision, he has an experience similar to one Ezekiel recorded.[1] In Reve-

[1] Ezekiel, at the beginning of his life as a prophet, had had a vision of the Lord. It included a voice of thunder and four living creatures that are similar to John's vision. Ezekiel was told to eat a scroll which the Lord gave him. Ezekiel ate it and described it as being sweet as honey. But then this sweet-tasting scroll was to become a very bitter message when he had to proclaim it to the people (Ezekiel 1:4—3:14).

lation 10:9, John is commanded to eat a scroll given him by an angel. He is told "it will be bitter in your stomach, but sweet as honey in your mouth" (10:9). He finds the words are true. Even as Ezekiel had the sweet experience of hearing the voice of God, but the bitter task of telling of the impending destruction, so John also has bitter words to say.

Apparently, the content of the message of the little scroll is what we find in chapter 11:1-13. John is told to measure—evidently to mark off rather than to find out how large it is—the area of the faithful. He is told that evil ones will have control of the rest of the holy city for 42 months. This is the same time period as the three and a half years of 12:14. Then John is told that two prophets will have power to prophesy for 1,260 days, the equivalent of 42 months or three and a half years. This stress on three and a half years as the duration of the greatest persecution comes originally from Daniel 7:25.

There has been a great deal of speculation among scholars concerning the identity of these two prophets. Revelation says, "I will give my two witnesses power to prophesy." Since two witnesses were required in Jewish law in order to attest to any word, some have thought this may simply refer to that sort of legal minimum, and not refer to two specific witnesses. Many others have identified these two witnesses with Moses and Elijah. There is good reason for this. Jewish thought before the time of Christ developed the idea that Moses or Elijah or both would reappear on the earth shortly before the coming of the Messiah. In the case of Elijah, this is prophesied in Malachi 4:5. For this reason some asked John the Baptist if he was Elijah (John 1:21). Jesus was also thought by some to be Elijah (Matthew 16:14). At the Transfiguration, both Elijah and Moses were seen standing with Jesus and Jesus implied that John the Baptist was to be identified with Elijah (Matthew 17:1-13). Also, the particular powers given to the two prophets mentioned in Revelation 11 are similar to the powers of Moses and Elijah.

There have also been attempts to identify the city in which these two are to prophesy. The references to the holy city and the temple make Jerusalem an easy choice. But in 11:8 mention is made of Sodom and Egypt. Yet it is also said that Christ was crucified there, so Jerusalem again is a candidate. The city may simply symbolize the whole earth in its rebellion against God.

Beyond any questions of identifying the city or these two prophets, the narration about them puts into bold relief what John has already implied about the fate of God's true witnesses. They have the strength from God to prophesy and to be faithful. Yet the beast gains power over them and they are killed. As a further insult to them, their bodies are left unburied in the streets.

The people rejoice at the deaths of the prophets for their words had been disturbing. The people are so glad to be rid of the prophets that they have parties and give gifts to each other in celebration. According to John, this is the fate of the faithful. They will be martyred. Then evil will rejoice and appear to be the victor.

But John's vision does not end here. It adds that three and a half days afterwards, these two witnesses will be given life again. They will hear a loud voice from heaven saying to them: "Come up hither!" In the sight of their foes, they will be taken up into heaven on a cloud. What is promised here is that the faithful prophet will join the risen and ascended Jesus Christ. The evil ones who have earlier thought themselves victors will be terrified. Some will be killed in the earthquake that follows. The others will give "glory to the God of heaven."

John is speaking only of the two prophets. But his words apply to all Christians. Those who remain faithful will share in the kingdom. They will hear their Lord's voice calling them and see him as victor over their enemies. John's vision encourages all of the faithful and promises them victory.

# Studying This Chapter

## Purpose of the Chapter

The purpose of this chapter is to show the character of the life of faith as seen by John. We do not live in the midst of severe trial and persecution, so the temptation to compromise our faith may seem small. Yet this very ease may mean that we give up trying to overcome evil when it seems too strong for us to change. John's words can guide us at this point. For the same reason, two elements of the Christian life are probably less significant for us than they were for John's hearers. The first of these is baptism. The second is prayer. Today we are also dealing with the use of women as symbols of good and evil in Revelation.

## Questions and Suggested Methods

1) Ask the members to share the lists they kept concerning the meaning of baptism. How do these responses compare with what John's original readers understood? Why is there a difference?

2) Divide the group into smaller units of four or five. Ask each group to define prayer, to discuss and

then write out a one-sentence answer to the question: How can we as members of a church help other members recapture the sense of prayer as being central to the Christian life? Come back together and share each group's answer.

3) Discuss the following questions: Is it true that we think it is useless to act unless things can be changed for the better by our actions? Are there situations in our own community that we know are evil and yet we have not done anything about them? Ask the group to list three or four, perhaps basing some of them on the work that was done in the last meeting. How does the Book of Revelation help us see that things can be done in spite of the seeming futility?

4) Review briefly the section in today's study on the figures of women. Which are most familiar to the group? Why do you think some of these figures are more familiar than others?

## Preparing for the Next Study

Our next study will deal with John's vision of God's ultimate goals for creation. Its purpose will be to seek ways in which we can give witness to that vision and act now out of that hope which we hold for the future. In the midst of the present struggle against evil, and in view of the victory of the Lamb, what are we to hope for? How are we to express that hope in our lives?

Those leading the group may wish to prepare the materials necessary for a discussion of question 2, at the end of that chapter, and also to be ready to teach "O Holy City, Seen of John" (The United Methodist Hymnal, #726) if it is not familiar to the group. (The words of this song are also in the next chapter.)

# 6
# A Vision
# of Newness

*Revelation 21:1—22:5*

Why is the Book of Revelation at the end of the Bible?

1. Some might think that this is due to the difficulty inherent in its interpretation. Indeed, some of the passages in this strange book can only be understood on the basis of a thorough acquaintance with biblical imagery and early Christian thought. For this reason one would do well to read the rest of the Bible first. But this is not the reason why this book appears at the end of the Bible.

2. Others believe that the Book of Revelation is a clue to the days in which we are living, so that each seal, each angel and each trumpet foretells events in the 20th century and that, for this reason, it appears at the end of the Bible. It is true that the Book of Revelation, as well as the rest of the Bible, speaks to our present situation. This is why we say that it is God's word to us. But as the fourth study demonstrated, any interpretation of this book as referring directly and exclusively to events in our day denies that it was the word of God for past generations.

3. Historically, one could say that at least one of

the reasons why the Book of Revelation appears at the end of the Bible is that it was one of the books which took longer to be universally accepted as scripture by the churches in various regions.

## A Book of Hope

There is a fundamental reason why the Book of Revelation is the last one in the Bible. That reason is simply that it is essentially a book of hope. Now, that seems strange to say about a book full of announcements of woe, where words such as "plague," "fire" and "wrath" abound. But the central message of this book is that evil has been conquered by the Lamb and that we are now witnessing the last great struggle. This is a message of hope. In spite of all the difficulties which we may have to face, we know that the One to whom we belong is the victor. Or, to use the vocabulary of Revelation, we know that our names are written "in the book of life."

What of the vast numbers of people who cringe in fear as they perceive in today's events signs they think are the beginning of the fulfillment of John's prophecies? Actually, they are in an odd situation, for Revelation actually says that those who truly believe have nothing to fear. This is a book of woe for those who serve the beast; but it is a book of hope for the chosen people who are sealed by the Lamb. Revelation says that there is no compromise possible. One must serve either the Lamb or the beast. As Jesus put it: "No one can serve two masters; for either he will hate the one and love the other, or he will be devoted to the one and despise the other. You cannot serve God and mammon" (Matthew 6:24). For those who serve the Lamb, there is no reason to fear, for Revelation is a book of Christian hope. For those who serve the beast, there is no reason to fear, for they presumably do not believe the message of Revelation.

The problem, however, is that many of us try to hedge on our bets. As John knew, the beast appears to be very powerful. Without serving it, people find life very difficult in today's world (Rev. 13:17). Thus, we may find ourselves both loving the beast and believing in John's words. This is not new. Augustine used to pray: "Lord, give me chastity; but not just now!" The Christians in the seven churches were also tempted and attracted by the power and prestige of the beast—that is precisely the reason why the Book of Revelation was necessary. This book does not appear to be a book of hope because it speaks of the utter futility and final destruction of much that we cherish—our own sinful inclinations, our world order, and even our civilization. Yet, the message of Revelation is that even beyond all this futility and destruction there stands One who has conquered death, and in whom we shall not taste "the second death."

Hope is like an empty drawer in which all sorts of things can be placed. People can "hope" to be rich, or to be happy, or to win games, or to see movies. Although hope is a Christian virtue, this is not true of all hopes. Even those who serve the beast "hope" that they will win. Therefore, when we say that Revelation is a book of hope we must immediately specify the content of that hope. What is it that a Christian is to hope for?

Once again at this point we must see the Book of Revelation in its place within the Bible. What this book hopes for is not something different from the hope of the patriarchs, the prophets, and the apostles. It is clear that Revelation is a counterpart to the account in Genesis about God's creation. Between the writing of Genesis and Revelation, there was a long history of a people whose expectations were grounded on Genesis and who looked forward to the final consummation of which Revelation speaks. This can be seen by comparing Revelation 21:1—22:5 with Genesis 2:7-10 and Ezekiel 47:1-12.

The Genesis narrative probably records one of Israel's most ancient traditions, dating from its beginnings as a people. Ezekiel's vision took place in one of Israel's saddest hours, when Jerusalem and its temple had been destroyed by Nebuchadrezzar. Ezekiel himself was in exile in Babylon.

As we compare these three passages, we are struck by the similar image of a flowing river. In Genesis we are told that "a river flowed out of Eden to water the garden, and there it divided and became four rivers." Ezekiel speaks of "water . . . issuing from below the threshold of the temple . . . and wherever the river goes every living creature which swarms will live." Finally, John says that the angel "showed me the river of the water of life, bright as crystal, flowing from the throne of God and of the Lamb, through the middle of the street of the city."

In every one of these passages, water is a symbol of life—as it is especially among peoples who have lived in relatively dry areas. This life flows out, not only within a limited area, but into the rest of the world. In Genesis the river becomes the four great rivers which bathe the land. In Ezekiel, the water which flows from the temple makes even the water of the sea fresh, "so everything will live where the river goes." In Revelation, we are not told that the river itself flows out of the city, but we are told that by the river stands the tree of life, and that "the leaves of the tree were for the healing of the nations." In conclusion, in all of these passages the imagery is that of an overflowing abundance of life which spills even beyond Eden, the temple, or the new Jerusalem. If this is to be our vision, perhaps we ought to think more seriously about our responsibilities in a world which cares little about justice, as nations and peoples deal with each other.

The parallelism with Ezekiel helps to explain two difficult phrases in Revelation. The first of these is John's assertion that "the sea was no more" (Rev. 21:1). In Ezekiel's vision, it becomes apparent that the sea is no more because the prophecy has been fulfilled. Ezekiel was probably drawing on the experience of the Dead Sea when he said that the waters from the river flowing from the temple would enter "the stagnant waters of the sea," which would then become fresh. John may have been drawing on his experience as an exile on an island, for whom the sea was a symbol of separation from his beloved Christian community. Both seers foretell the destruction of all that is stagnant and alienating by the power flowing from God.

The other puzzling phrase appears in Revelation 22:2, where it says "on either side of the river, the tree of life . . ." What can be meant by a tree growing on either side of a river? It is difficult to imagine such a thing. For this reason, some interpreters have suggested that the term "tree" is really speaking of several trees. But this would destroy the parallelism with the Genesis narrative, which is very strong here. If, on the other hand, we read John's vision in connection with Ezekiel's, the meaning of this phrase becomes clearer: just as Ezekiel saw water flowing below the threshold of the temple, John saw it flowing *through* the tree of life. In John's vision, Genesis and Ezekiel are brought together. What does all this mean? It means that God's love, from which life flows, is expansive. God did not create Eden in order to have a happy Adam and Eve live there, while the rest of the earth suffered in thirst. God would not restore the temple so that the faithful remnant of the Jewish people could be nourished in it, while the rest of the world remained dead and stagnant. God will not create a new Jerusalem apart from "the healing of the nations."

Being aware of this idea of God's expansive love is most important for a balanced understanding of the message of the Book of Revelation. Evil is real. Since it is real, God will neither ignore it nor let it remain forever. God's wrath is neither a figment of the imagination nor a convenient way to explain that which we do not like. Since evil and God's wrath are real, there must be conflict. The Book of Revelation is full of conflict. But John's final vision, which goes beyond the present conflict, speaks of "the healing of the nations"—that is, of God's love, flowing out like the river of Eden in Genesis, or like the river reaching the four corners of the earth in Ezekiel.

Another interesting comparison has to do with the temple. In the Genesis passage, there obviously is no temple for Genesis speaks of a time when human beings had direct communion with God. When Ezekiel had his vision, the temple had been destroyed and many despaired that Israel would ever be restored to her earlier joy and freedom. Thus, Ezekiel's vision spoke a word of hope to Israel and, at the same time, a word of warning that the restoration would not be only for her own good. Revelation goes beyond this vision of Ezekiel and points to the restoration of God's original purpose, when John says "I saw no temple in the city, for its temple is the Lord God the Almighty and the Lamb" (Rev. 21:22).[1]

---

[1] This may relate to Jeremiah's promise (Jer. 31:31-34) of a new time when God's covenant would be written in human hearts, and the knowledge of God would no longer have to be taught by people to each other.

We stand neither at the point of Genesis nor at the fulfillment of John's vision. We still need a "temple." We still need to be taught about God by each other. We still need a community of faith—a church. Thus, we stand closer to the situation of Ezekiel. Through God's grace, a "temple" has been given us. Ezekiel calls us to remember that out of the temple must flow water which will freshen every stagnant sea "so everything will live where the river goes." We hope for the day when there will be no temple, for the day when God becomes our temple.

## A New Jerusalem

The holy city is called "new Jerusalem" in Revelation 21:2. An important element in John's Christian hope is hope for the fulfillment of the promises made to Israel. As the church became increasingly Gentile and less Jewish and as conflicts flared with orthodox Jews, many in the church began to think of Jews as an apostate people who had forfeited the promises made to them. This is certainly not the position of the Book of Revelation, which is firmly grounded in the Jewish tradition.

When the heavenly city is called "new Jerusalem" it means that this new creation is the fulfilment of God's promises to Abraham and his descendants. It is the fulfilment of the vision of prophets such as Ezekiel, Jeremiah and Isaiah—all of whom looked forward to the restoration of Jerusalem to a place of preeminence among the nations.

This can also be seen in the text: the city is surrounded by "a great, high wall, with twelve gates, and at the gates twelve angels, and on the gates the names of the twelve tribes of the sons of Israel were inscribed" (21:12). The 12 tribes are not simply something of the past, to be forgotten as we move on to better things. They are part of God's intended future for humankind, of the new Jerusalem. At each of the 12 gates is an angel. We are immediately reminded of Genesis 3:24: after the fall, God drove Adam and Eve out of the garden, "and at the east of the garden of Eden he placed the cherubim, and a flaming sword which turned every way, to guard the way to the tree of life." Likewise, here in the heavenly city the tree of life is surrounded by "a great, high wall," whose 12 gates are guarded by 12 angels. Presumably, none can enter into the holy city without going through one of these gates which are inscribed with the names of the tribes of Israel. Or, in other words, none can enter the city without becoming a child of Abraham.

We tend to think of the city of John's vision as if it were the totality of God's plan for creation. When the heavenly city comes, there will be nothing else. However, this is not what John saw. His vision included not only a heavenly city but also a new heaven and a new earth. Presumably the holy city is not the only nation left, for Revelation 21:24 says: "By its light shall the nations walk; and the kings of the earth shall bring their glory into it." Also, its gates will always be open (21:25), which implies coming and going in and out of the city. The tree of life in the midst of it produces leaves "for the healing of the nations" (22:2).[2]

Exactly what this means is impossible to tell. But one thing is certain: the Book of Revelation depicts God's final purpose in grand tones which confound all our preconceived images and classifications.

---

[2] All of this reminds us of the visions of the prophets of the Old Testament, where the hope of Israel was that Jerusalem would be a light for all the nations, and all kings would honor her. See, for instance, Isaiah 49:8-26, Jeremiah 33:10-16, and Micah 4:1-5.

# A Heavenly City

John's vision is of a *city*. In our modern times we are so overwhelmed by the problems of our cities that we find it difficult to conceive that God's ultimate purposes may best be described as centering on a city. We prefer to think in terms of the peace, quiet, and privacy of the country, where we don't have to deal with all the baffling problems of human relations. Sometimes we even find support for this in Isaiah's vision of the peaceable kingdom, where all sorts of beasts live together in peace and are led by a small child. The imagery in Isaiah is more rural than that in Revelation. However, the prophet did not speak of each beast going its own way and not bothering the other but of a harmonious animal society.

Again, John's vision is of a *city*. This should not surprise us for, in his time and throughout the early history of the Church, Christianity was an urban religion. Many of these cities were places of fierce competition where Christians, who were mostly slaves or poor people, did not have an easy time. These Christians did not hope for an end to all cities, when all would be able to live in country villas or in summer homes like the rich. Their hope was for a new ordering of city life, where God would "wipe away every tear from their eyes," and death would cease (Rev. 21:4). Furthermore, the city which John saw was no small country town, for it measured "twelve thousand stadia" in each direction—that is, about 1,500 miles! The area covered by this city would make the Boston-New York-Philadelphia-Baltimore-Washington complex look like a small town! And that is without even counting the height of the city, another 1,500 miles, which would make the Empire State Building look like a cabin.

Obviously, the dimensions are not to be taken literally, but they do point to a fact that we often forget. The Bible does not depict God's plans for humankind basically in terms of individual privacy, but rather in terms of one vast community where all will live with each other in peace and justice. This is why the imagery most often used is that of a city or a kingdom. Both are entities in which citizens relate to each other. The Bible nowhere speaks of the redeemed as floating around on private clouds, playing their own private music on a golden harp. The Bible speaks of cities and kingdoms, and when it speaks of music, it speaks of choirs.

## A New Heaven and a New Earth

The holy city of John's vision is part of an entirely new creation (12:1). As we read this verse, we may be surprised that not only earth but also heaven have to be made anew. Part of our surprise may be due to the fact that we are used to thinking in terms of a good heaven, unspoiled by evil, and an earth in which the struggle takes place. But the Book of Revelation gives us an entirely different view. Satan's abode was in heaven, until he was cast down, not directly by his sin, but by the Lamb's victory. Therefore heaven, no less than earth, has been corrupted by evil. The struggle has already taken place in heaven, and that is precisely why the struggle has become more fierce on earth. Evil is not limited to one particular sphere of creation. Therefore the Lamb and its followers must fight it on earth and in heaven.

Also, we tend to think that evil is connected with our earthliness. If we were pure spirits, we would do no evil. If we could only be heavenly creatures, rather than earthly ones, we would not sin. Yet, scripture tells us plainly that the chief forces of evil are heavenly creatures. Thus, the root of evil is not to be found in our material nature or in the fact that we have bodies. It is to be found in the will which rebels against God's purposes and which can then turn both earth and heaven into battlefields.

In any case, what we have here is not a vision that earth will become heavenly, but rather that both earth and heaven will be made anew by the One who says "Behold, I make all things new." Here again we can see the Book of Revelation as the counterpart of Genesis. In the Genesis narrative, the earth is cursed, not because it is material, but because of sin (Gen. 3:17). Here in Revelation, because of the victory of the Lamb, earth is created anew.

What does this mean for us? Often we think that the Gospel has to do only with "spiritual" realities and that God's purposes have to do only with getting us to heaven. But here God's purposes include the restoration of both heaven *and earth*. If we call ourselves followers of the Lamb—if we are among those that bear its seal—as those who share in John's hope and vision, we must deal with the earth and with each other. We must not be a curse upon the earth, polluting it with waste and pesticides. And we must not, for the sake of our own comfort and privacy, turn our backs on those with whom we hope to live in the coming great city.

## Epilogue

We do not know exactly what happened to John after he wrote his visions. Indications are that when Domitian died in A.D. 96, John was allowed to leave

Patmos and return to Ephesus, where he died around the year 100. Later, legends developed around him. One was that the Roman authorities tried to fry him in oil and he came out of the ordeal unharmed. Another legend recorded by St. Augustine was that he had not really died, for if one looked attentively at his sepulchre in Ephesus one could see that the earth heaved. This was considered to be a sign that John was still breathing!

Whatever may have happened to John himself, one thing is certain: his vision still stands. Since the new heaven and the new earth of which he spoke have not yet come, we are still in the struggle against the last stand of the powers of evil.

And yet, things have changed since John's time. Not only did Domitian die, but so did all the others who persecuted the church. Eventually, in the fourth century, Constantine and his successors turned the situation around. Becoming a Christian no longer meant choosing to be an outcast of society but a respectable citizen. After the empire became the ally of the church, some attacked the Book of Revelation because it called Rome a harlot and did not show great respect for the civil authorities. John's visions and warnings seemed valuable for a time of persecution but not for a time of freedom to preach, of tax exemption for the church, and of Christians in high places. All of this began with Constantine.

Yet, John's words were just as applicable in this latter situation—which is also ours—for he repeatedly warns us of the danger of compromise. The struggle did not end when Christianity became respectable. On the contrary, it shifted to another flank. Now we are tempted to worship the power of evil, not because there is persecution but because there is so much ease. The Bible tells about God's call for love and justice among races and nations, but we often find that to speak the word or take the action required by such knowledge would endanger our standing in society. We are consuming an inordinate proportion of the earth's bounty. With our greed and waste we are cursing the earth which God intends to bless. We know these things. And we also know from the Book of Revelation that we are to bear either the mark of the beast or the seal of the Lamb. Which will it be? The question is as simple as that. The question is also as difficult as that.

## Studying This Chapter

### Purpose of the Chapter

Our actions are usually guided by our goals and hopes. If we wish to reach a certain city, we try to get on the road which leads to it. If we hope to be able to buy something, we start saving money to that end. Likewise, in the Christian life, much of what we are and do now is guided by what we hope to become, or where we hope to be. For this reason it is important to clarify that for which Christians hope.

Too often we imagine a heaven of quiet privacy, where we shall not have to relate to others but only to God. Such a vision leads to a religion where private devotion is deemed sufficient, where little is said about responsibility to social conditions around us. But the hope of John's vision was different. His was a vision of a city where all live together in love and justice—his was a vision of radical urban renewal! This being the case, if we as Christians are to be guided in our present life by the nature of our future hope, we must *now* begin seeking ways to relate to each other as citizens of that new Jerusalem, with love and justice for all.

## Questions and Suggested Methods

1) Sing or read "O Holy City, Seen of John" in *The United Methodist Hymnal*. Do we mean these words? If so, what can we do to put that belief in action?

# O Holy City, Seen of John

1. O holy city, seen of John,
   Where Christ, the Lamb, doth reign,
   Within whose four-square walls shall come
   No night, nor need, nor pain,
   And where the tears are wiped from eyes
   That shall not weep again!

2. Hark, how from men whose lives are held
   More cheap than merchandise,
   From women struggling sore for bread,
   From little children's cries,
   There swells the sobbing human plaint
   That bids thy walls arise!

2) If you live in a city or a large town where there are several churches of our denomination, make a list of those churches. How many of them are actually in the downtown area? How many *new* churches are there in that area? In what parts of town are our churches growing? Does this situation give a witness to our community that is faithful to John's vision? If so, how can we make that witness clearer and stronger? If not, what can we do about it?

3. O shame to us who rest content
   while lust and greed for gain
   In street and shop and tenement
   Wring gold from human pain,
   And bitter lips in blind despair
   Cry, "Christ hath died in vain!"

4. Give us, O God, the strength to build
   The city that hath stood
   Too long a dream, whose laws are love,
   Whose crown is servanthood,
   And where the sun that shineth is
   God's grace for human good.

5. Already in the mind of God
   That city riseth fair:
   Lo, how its splendor challenges
   The souls that greatly dare,
   Yea, bids us seize the whole of life
   And build its glory there.          *Amen.*

3) Who are some groups in our own community with whom we do not feel comfortable? Is there someone we would not like to have as a next door neighbor or as a member of our congregation? Are we certain that this person, or persons, is not intended to be our neighbor in the new Jerusalem? Can we honestly refuse to have such a person as a neighbor here on earth and still claim that we are Christians who share John's vision?

4) Because this is the last of our chapters, ask the group which part of the whole study has been the most significant or challenging for them. In addition, suggest that each of them, very soon, read again the whole Book of Revelation and see if it now looks different to them.

# For Further Study

As we have suggested throughout this book, the best companion for the study of the Book of Revelation is the rest of the Bible, for it is from the Bible that most of its imagery is drawn. Its theology also reflects strains in Jewish and early Christian thought which can be found in other parts of scripture.

The use and comparison of different translations may be valuable. But beware of paraphrases such as *The Living Bible,* which in many cases, in an attempt to clarify the original Greek text, depart drastically from it. All of our quotations have been taken from the *Revised Standard Version* since this is the one most commonly used in our churches. But, in many instances, the Jerusalem Bible has helpful translations and notes.

There are many commentaries on the Book of Revelation. Some are so detailed and technical that the reader may be lost in the maze of their information and arguments. The one which we have found most helpful is *I Saw a New Earth,* by Paul S. Minear (Washington: Corpus Books, 1968). We also recommend *The Interpreter's Bible,* Vol. XII, particularly the essay which appears on pages 551-613, "The Message of the Book of Revelation." The reader may also find significant help in G. B. Caird's *The Revelation of St. John the Divine* (New York: Harper & Row, 1966), which is part of *Harper's New Testament Commentaries.* A scholar of the last generation, noted for his expertise on apocalyptic material, was R. H. Charles, who wrote the two volumes on Revelation for *The International Critical Commentary* (New York: Charles Scribner's Sons, 1920). These volumes are excellent, somewhat dated on matters of detail, but may be too technical and involved for the average reader.

For the geography of Asia Minor and the letters to the seven churches, the following books will be helpful: William Barclay, *Letters to Seven Churches* (Nashville: Abingdon Press, 1957); A. H. M. Jones, *The Cities of the Eastern Roman Empire,* 2nd ed. (Oxford: Clarendon Press, 1971); W. M. Ramsay, *The Letters to the Seven Churches in Asia and their Place in the Plan of the Apocalypse* (New York: Hodder & Stoughton, n. d.).

Throughout this book we have emphasized the liturgical connections of the Book of Revelation. In this respect the reader may wish to consult Oscar Cullmann, *Early Christian Worship* (London: SCM Press, 1953), and Massey H. Shepherd, Jr. *The Paschal Liturgy and the Apocalypse* (Richmond, Va.: John Knox Press, 1960).

Finally, on the general theme of apocalyptic literature, see H. H. Rowley, *The Relevance of Apocalyptic* (New York: Harper, 1955); D. S. Russell, *Method and Message of Jewish Apocalyptic* (Philadelphia: Westminster Press, 1964); and Paul S. Minear, *New Testament Apocalyptic* (Nashville: Abingdon Press, 1981).

# Glossary

**Apocalypse:** a title often used for the Book of Revelation: The Apocalypse. It comes directly from a Greek word for revelation or unveiling and, more specifically, revelation about what is to happen at the end of this age.

**Apocalyptic:** a term used to describe a certain way of viewing the events expected at the end of this age. It includes the belief that evil is now allowed to go unchecked in this world because God is about to end this age and judge between the righteous and the unrighteous.

**Apocalyptic Literature:** writings which are concerned with the expectation of the end of this age which is near, and the events that are to take place. Such literature arises during times of persecution. It helps to answer the question: Why is God allowing the righteous to suffer? It answers this question by showing that God is about to intervene and end the age, punishing evil and rewarding those who are faithful now. The present is therefore a time of testing. The Book of Revelation is an example of apocalyptic literature.

**Didache:** *The Didache of the Twelve Apostles* is a very early Christian writing, dating from the late first or early second century. It contains many directions for Christian worship, including the communion service. The word *didache* is a Greek word meaning "teachings."

**Eschatology:** is a technical theological term for doctrines concerning "the last things" or the end of the age. It comes from a Greek word meaning "the end" or "the last." Eschatology and apocalypse are concerned with the end. Eschatology is the more general term and does not necessarily include the elements listed above under "apocalyptic literature."

**Eschatological Literature:** writings which deal with what is to be expected at the end of this present age. This is a more general term than apocalyptic literature. All apocalyptic literature can also be called eschatological literature, but not all eschatological literature is apocalyptic. (See above: "Eschatology")

**II Esdras:** an apocalyptic book of about the same date as the Book of Revelation. It was originally written by a Jew, but later some additions were made by Christians. The name "Esdras" is the Greek form of the Hebrew name Ezra. This book can be found in some Bibles, such as *The New Oxford Annotated Bible with the Apocrypha.* In many Roman Catholic editions, the Old Testament books of Ezra and Nehemiah are called I and II Esdras. In these cases, what is called II Esdras in this study book becomes IV Esdras.

**Free City:** a town whose citizens had been granted Roman citizenship. At the time of Revelation, all the towns of Italy were free cities, and therefore all free Italians were Roman citizens. But in other parts of the Roman Empire most people and most towns did not enjoy such privileges. The citizens of a free city also had a certain degree of autonomy, and could elect some of their officials.

**Imagery:** figurative language that creates pictures in the mind in order to convey a message. The message is misunderstood when such language is taken literally.

**Kingdom of God:** a term frequently used for the joyful expectation of what God intends at the end of this age. It implies not only the rule of God, unopposed by evil, but also the corporate character of this hope. A kingdom implies people related to each other as a society. This same idea is conveyed by the term "City of God."

**Maranatha:** words in Aramaic, one of the languages of first century Palestine, which mean "Our Lord, come!" or "Our Lord comes!" or "Our Lord has come!" These words, found in Revelation 22:20, were also used in communion services in the early church.

**Martyr:** from a Greek word meaning "witness." About the time the Book of Revelation was written, this word was acquiring the more specific meaning within the church of one who was a faithful witness to Christ, to the point of death.

**Messiah:** Hebrew term for "anointed one" which in Greek is translated "Christ." For Christians, the term is most appropriately used for Jesus. For this reason it is the title of George Frederick Handel's great oratorio, *Messiah*. This work is the musical setting of many biblical passages, including some from the Book of Revelation.

**Messianic Community:** the people of Israel from whom the Messiah was to come. It can also be used for the church, the community of faith which comes into being because of the Messiah.

**Millenium:** a period of a thousand years. In regard to the Book of Revelation, it refers to the period of peace lasting a thousand years which is mentioned in chapter 20.

**Numbers:** see "Symbolism."

**Post-millenialists:** Christians who expect the return of Christ at the end of the thousand-year period mentioned in Revelation 20.

**Pre-millenialists:** Christians who expect the return of Christ at the beginning of the thousand-year period mentioned in Revelation 20.

**Prophecy:** the message of a prophet. Although sometimes it refers to the future, in other cases it is an interpretation of a past or present situation.

**Prophet:** in the Old Testament, one of the people chosen by God to speak God's word to the people of God. In the New Testament, prophets are inspired men and women who speak to the people when the church gathers for worship. The author of Revelation may have been such a prophet.

**Symbolism:** The use of a word or sign that is given significance far beyond its literal meaning because of ideas or emotions that have become associated with the word or sign. In the Book of Revelation, many numbers are used as symbols. Three and a half is usually a negative symbol. Based on the Book of Daniel, it represents a time of tribulation—particularly in Revelation 11 and 12. Six can sometimes have a positive meaning, especially when it is seen as three pairs—as in the case of the seraphim in Isaiah 6:2. But in Revelation it usually denotes imperfection, for it lacks one for the perfect number, seven. Seven, ten, and twelve are positive numbers, symbolizing perfection. Creation was complete on the seventh day, God's commandments are ten, and both the tribes of Israel and the apostles of the church were twelve. The most common numbers used symbolically in Revelation are 6, 7, and 12.